MW00719365

United Nations Security Council Permanent Member Perspectives

This book is part of the Peter Lang Politics and Economics list.
Every volume is peer reviewed and meets
the highest quality standards for content and production.

PETER LANG
New York • Bern • Berlin
Brussels • Vienna • Oxford • Warsaw

John Michael Weaver

United Nations Security Council Permanent Member Perspectives

Implications for U.S. and Global Intelligence Professionals

PETER LANG
New York • Bern • Berlin
Brussels • Vienna • Oxford • Warsaw

Library of Congress Cataloging-in-Publication Control Number: 2018052104

Bibliographic information published by **Die Deutsche Nationalbibliothek**.
Die Deutsche Nationalbibliothek lists this publication in the "Deutsche
Nationalbibliografie"; detailed bibliographic data are available
on the Internet at http://dnb.d-nb.de/.

ISBN 978-1-4331-5925-1 (hardback: alk. paper)
ISBN 978-1-4331-5943-5 (ebook pdf)
ISBN 978-1-4331-5945-9 (epub)
ISBN 978-1-4331-6428-6 (mobi)
DOI 10.3726/b15317

© 2019 Peter Lang Publishing, Inc., New York
29 Broadway, 18th floor, New York, NY 10006
www.peterlang.com

TABLE OF CONTENTS

Chapter 1: Background Information   1
Chapter 2: Research Questions, Methodology, and Limitations   11
Chapter 3: United Nations (Context)   21
Chapter 4: The United States (an Overview of Priorities)   25
Chapter 5: China   33
Chapter 6: France   49
Chapter 7: Russia   63
Chapter 8: United Kingdom   77
Chapter 9: Analysis and Findings   89
Chapter 10: Conclusion   99

Index   103
About the Author   107

· 1 ·

BACKGROUND INFORMATION

Since the ending of the Cold War in 1991, the world has seen reduced travel restrictions, the proliferation of commercial air travel, and access to most countries (for example throughout much of the European Union) as a result of globalization, the relaxation of impediments to imports and exports, and the continuance of free markets. What has ensued has been weakened border security where it is tepid at best to nonexistent at worst. Subsequently, it has allowed for ease of movement for nefarious types employed in drug and human trafficking businesses, cross border illegal arms sales, the transit of counterfeit goods, and the movement of terrorists and their organizations with the follow-on establishment of their cells.

Those involved in national intelligence should see this as a concern. Intelligence community (IC) members (particularly those that are allies with the United States) must strive for greater situational awareness with regards to what is occurring and not just within their own organizations, but what is taking place throughout non-intelligence sectors of government as well as the world at large (Weaver, 2016). When leaders make decisions, the outcomes could be profound; there may be unintended secondary and tertiary effects on efforts occurring both within one's country and the contiguous nations and regions beyond their sphere of influence especially in the realm of intelligence collection when looking to globalization's impact. Policy makers and intelligence professionals alike will have to work with one another to overcome challenges between the two (Jervis, 2010, p. 203). Particularly, this is seen as true when considering countries as a primary unit of analysis in the context of international relations (Lamy, Masker, Baylis, & Owens, 2015). More pointedly, with communication allowing for the proliferation of messaging, as communication fosters the burgeoning of information, and as economic transformation occurs in the backdrop to globalization, intelligence leaders will have to "think globally as they act locally" (Lamy et al., 2015). IC members, in the conduct of their activities with policy makers, will need to work together to generate requirements during the first phase of the intelligence cycle, and as they look further the next phase when moving to activities centered on collection (and collection platform tasking) (Lowenthal, 2015). What becomes increasingly apparent is a need to afford greater consideration to a more comprehensive and global perspective.

Consider the United Nations (U.N.); dialog among the U.N. Security Council's permanent members is quite complicated (Weaver, 2016). The U.N. has undergone extensive changes over the years and has seemingly improved its efficiency as it has conducted business (GAO/T-NSIAD-99-196, 1999). Contemplate the Iranian nuclear program and what transpired throughout the summer of 2015. It was seemingly understandable that all five permanent Security Council members were congruous in their pursuit of a homogeneous approach in their attempt to thwart this country in its effort to develop a nuclear weapon (Obama, 2015). All five wanted to halt it of the uranium enrichment program; all had a desire to reward Iran through the walking back of sanctions for irrefutable actions and behavior that was favorable to the permanent members as was evident through the actual agreement's implementation.

Nevertheless, what appears as an integrated effort in one part of the world does not necessarily transcend to other locations and senior intelligence leaders should have an appreciation for this (Weaver, 2016). The Ukrainian security crisis currently underscores this. Since the fall of 2014, escalation of tensions has resulted in Russia annexing Crimea and with the continuation of this country to provide Russian backed rebels with materiel support necessary to wreak havoc throughout Ukraine to the consternation of the United States (U.S.), most of Europe, and many other allies throughout the world (DOD Press Briefing, 2015).

Even though the U.S. and other permanent security members required unanimity (Russia notwithstanding) on the Iranian nuclear program, here the non-Russian western members of the U.N. Security Council regard Russia as a potent antagonist. North Atlantic Treaty Organization (NATO) member countries (with great contribution by U.S. forces) have even gone as far as participating in Atlantic Resolve, a show of force exercise in Eastern Europe (in former Warsaw Pact countries). Among the activities, these have included the deployment of Army tank and mechanized forces to Latvia, A-10 attack aircraft to Romania, F-15 fighter jets to Bulgaria; the U.S. even has a training force in Ukraine ostensibly to assist in education of the country's guardsmen (Weaver, 2016). All of this is intended to showcase to Russia that the United States and her allies still have capacity to project forces even though many of these countries are still actively engaged with operations in the U.S. Central Command area of operations to include Afghanistan, Iraq, Syria and other countries.

What's more, is that NATO in general (and more specifically the United Kingdom, and France with the United States - three of the five permanent U.N. Security members) is poised to implement the Very High Joint Readiness Task Force (VJTF) as a direct corollary to Russia's forays into Ukraine thereby building on initiatives previously developed under the NATO Response Force (NRF) construct brought to fruition early in the millennium (Weaver, 2016).

These exercises and developments are underpinned by the necessitation of heterogeneous allied intelligence organizations focusing collection efforts to better assess Russia's intentions at home in the context of what is occurring elsewhere throughout the globe. What's more is that efforts to implement Ukrainian training initiatives can be used to further the gathering and collection on Russia, the latest tactics, techniques, and procedures (TTPs) employed by the Russian backed rebels, and her equipment capabilities.

China is another behemoth actor on the world stage (Weaver, 2018a). Many countries see this country's brazen asymmetrical operations, vis-à-vis cyber, as a potential world security destabilizer in general, and global interests focused on its own economic security more specifically (Weaver, 2016). Likewise, China's meddling in cyberspace threatens not just governments but allegedly she is actively involved in the exploitation of proprietary information, and data the world over for its own narcissistic intentions (ISAB, 2015). These attacks allegedly have included the hacking of human rights activists' Gmail accounts recently, intrusion into Google's network in 2010, and the Sony attack in late 2014 (Lamy et al., 2015). Those that work for the various intelligence organizations that have sharing relations with the United States continue to try to discern China's objective in an effort to construct and put in place viable defensive countermeasures to thwart future hacking attempts all in the backdrop of economic globalization.

China's military muscle flexing has occurred in the South China Sea (Weaver, 2018b). Specifically, it has escalated its naval activity and presence over the last several years in this body of water. Moreover, it has obtained and upgraded a Russian aircraft carrier, and actively pursued land reclamation projects as it builds airstrips and other military facilities and structures throughout the Spratly Islands (Lamy et al., 2015). Though with the latter, under the auspices of improving its reliability of weather forecasts, China has claimed that this is its true reason for building up a presence on these islands. A direct spin off of Chinese endeavors has been the implementation of a joint exercise by the U.S., the Philippines, and Japan in the regional waterways, though apparently as a way to enhance disaster preparatory efforts is actually a show of force exercise designed to demonstrate resolve of Asian influencers in concert with the United States in the South China Sea. Arguably, it could be a way for these countries to also gather information on China through this "reconnaissance by force" initiative.

Additionally, the United States, Russia, and others in Northeast Asia require Chinese support. They still need China's leverage emanating from its close relationship as a staunch supporter to North Korea to apply pressure to this rogue nation with the intent to move it away from nuclear weapons' development, the testing of long range ballistic missile technology (now capable of reaching parts of the U.S.), and the proliferation and exportation of said materiel and knowledge to other questionable nations like Syria (Lamy et al., 2015). This underscores the challenges confronting career intelligence professionals as they try to un-package the complexities of relationships and actions to better ascertain China's long-term aspirations.

Just on the other side of the border of Iraq where the U.S. presence has escalated in recent years, the United States has a unique relationship with Iran as Hassan Rouhani's forces have fought the Islamic State of Iraq and Syria (ISIS) in Iraq. This formidable enemy at its peak had an estimated 20,000 fighters between Iraq and Syria and historically has operated in large swaths of both countries with near impunity (Quinlan, 2014). The U.S. in its current "train and assist" mission hasn't served as a viable countermeasure to prevent Iran from engaging in direct combat with ISIS in Iraq (White House Briefing, 2015). More pointedly, the United States had actually openly encouraged Iran to maintain and keep its lines of communications open with the Iraqi government in an effort to deconflict activities and to coordinate military efforts. Yet the relationship, with regards to Iran, is more tepid in Yemen where it is seen as an alleged backer of the Houthi rebels there. This is a great concern to senior officials of the United States and by extension its counterterrorism efforts in that country, especially since it has been largely perceived until recent times as the textbook way on how to conduct counter-terrorism operations. Once again, the IC has its work cut out for it as these organizations try to understand the overall direction of Iran chiefly in the backdrop of the approved nuclear agreement with Iran and its desire to enter into the globalization frenzy as sanctions continue to ease.

These issues and more provide challenges to world security and peace. Clear examples of the challenges in today's world, to the U.N. Security Council, other global leaders and, senior public officials (particularly with those whose decisions have an impact beyond the country's interior affairs) and by extension the members of the IC are showcased in numerous events (Weaver, 2016). These include ISIS and its presence and exerted influence in Syria, Iraq, and now Afghanistan, the recent fall of the government in Yemen, and humanitarian challenges posed by Boko Haram's influence in Nigeria. This is salient when turning towards the United States' hegemonic position which is seemingly diminishing with each passing year and through the proliferation of globalization (and associated inextricable linkages among nation states). Senior leaders within the IC focusing collection efforts must try to understand decisional effects and not just within a single country, but what the impact could have regionally and across the globe during times when some of those countries are expressly allied with the United States and other nations where there are relationships of convenience for specific purposes (especially in some instances when other actors can be perceived as potential antagonists in other scenarios). This importance increases when looking to what cascading effects a leader's decision will have not just on specific countries but world events in general as those influencers articulate national interests and implement foreign policy to foster their ideas and positions (Lamy et al., 2015).

The U.S. military has subscribed to using the diplomatic, informational, military, and economic ("D.I.M.E.") instruments of national power for years (Weaver, 2018b, p. 63). Historically, these have assisted in guiding senior intelligence leaders through the application of a clearly defined mission statement. Its articulation and promulgation throughout their organizations and others in their own national intelligence organizations, as well as those intelligence agencies with information sharing arrangements to the United States (Wilcox, 2010). As intelligence professionals consider these four instruments, these instruments could assist them in the critical thinking process with just how decisions in one area affect those in another notably in the backdrop to globalization all while gauging how the other permanent members of the United Nations Security Council might act. Likewise, one can hope to achieve a level of synergy through a more comprehensive and multilateral approach to issues moving beyond one's own country or region and the subsequent impact potentially made beyond their purview (Weaver, 2018a). This is particularly relevant in the requirements generation and the collection phases of the intelligence cycle.

Diplomatically, U.S. leader engagement in foreign policy has looked at efforts to help realize the strategic goals of this country. This entails not just the applicability of policy to one specific country but rather it should also look regionally at effects that decisions will have in surrounding countries and even beyond (Weaver & Pomeroy, 2016). Often there is a proclivity towards diplomacy over military intervention provided that it is used correctly; diplomacy can help shape the environment bringing about agreeable outcomes to countries adept at using this instrument (Weaver, 2018b). Moreover, it could be far less expensive in terms of long term costs by engaging diplomatically and the long term positive impacts that could emanate from sound, well-thought decisions on the world economy and more pointedly, globalization. When turning to diplomacy in shaping issues, the intelligence community has tried to predict whether or not members of the UNSC will back initiatives set forth by their nations based on what the Security Council member might gain or lose through such policy initiatives. What's more is that senior intelligence leaders must know that diplomacy does not operate in a vacuum and should consider the other instruments of power and what effects could be realized in these areas as well.

Information as an instrument through proper messaging is critical to the conduct of business; this applies not just in the private industry, but in the public-sector fields as well (especially at the federal governmental level). Senior intelligence professional (civilians and military alike) must strive to frame issues factually in the hopes to sell to the public (both at home and abroad) on how and why it is going about conducting its business; this is necessary in order to maintain credibility and sense of legitimacy especially as it seeks the support of the other Security Council permanent members (Weaver, 2016). Interestingly, this is the least expensive instrument of power and one that can just as easily be used by all countries (not just the wealthy) and non-state actors alike (to include organizations like ISIS) against another country or non-state actor. Leaders must understand that parity exists concerning the use of information and must strive to successfully undertake steps in order to better legitimize one's position while working to undermine that of an adversary. Accordingly, like the diplomatic instrument of power, it cannot be used autonomously and should be applied with the other instruments (Weaver, 2016).

The instrument of power that is probably best known and that is often referred to as "hard power" is the military (Weaver, 2016). The implementation includes the following: show of force exercises, the employment of humanitarian relief teams, peacekeeping forces, peace enforcement operations, and full-on combat. Arguably, the U.S. still possess the best funded & resourced and most robust military capability in the world even as it has experienced downsizing in recent years (though, this trend is changing).

That stated, even the United States has felt significant strain in recent years with regards to forces deployed predominately to Afghanistan and Iraq, as well as other enduring missions that have lasted decades such as the military personnel assigned to the Republic of Korea and its forward presence in Europe. Those that work in the intelligence profession have come to terms with this and also use the military as a way to test the counter actions of potential foes and leverage the intelligence that they are gathering on site to provide a more accurate common operational picture with regards to what is playing out on the world stage. As is the case with the two aforementioned instruments, it could benefit one's country by acquiring the support of the permanent members of the Security Council. Conversely, leaders (to include the intelligence community) must try to forecast if a member or members of the Security Council will oppose or attempt to suppress military intervention thereby weakening the county's position of legitimacy that is considering using this instrument. What is concerning in contemporary times is the rising military tensions the world over (WEF, 2018, p. 7).

Money underpins almost everything and is seen as equated to power (Weaver, 2016). Economics historically has been used as a way to cajole leaders, organizations, and governments for centuries. Nations can exert influence economically by using the power of the purse coercively. In recent years though there has been concern about bilateral trade wars and multilateral disputes occurring which could lead to greater economic instability throughout the world (WEF, 2018, p. 28). Whether allocating rewards for favorable behavior (i.e., preferential import/export arrangements that pertain to a specific country) or through the use of more assertive practices (embargos and sanctions), senior leaders have to understand how this can help influence behavior more in stride with what the nation's objectives are and just how the

IC can understand and predict outcomes of economic leverage through analysis on the behavior of targeted countries. What's more, success can be better realized if the IC can adequately predict responses of the permanent members of the UNSC when considering what each of these counties stand to lose or gain by the imposition of economic pressure.

The United Nations met in New York on September 19th of 2017; during the General Session, President Trump addressed world leaders (Trump, 2017). During his speech he made reference to challenges confronting world order to include the likes of terrorism, extremism, rogue regimes, weapons of mass destruction and more. To address these issues, he called on the sovereign nations of the world to work together to promote greater security, prosperity, and peace for the people of the planet; in particular he called on the U.N. to serve as a conveyance for this through the strength and resolve of the independent nations that make up this body (Trump, 2017). China, France, Russia, the U.K. and the U.S. will have challenges in the foreseeable future to deal with arising problems.

References

DOD Press Briefing. (2015). *DOD Press Briefing on April 16, 2015 with Secretary of Defense Carter and GEN Dempsey.* http://www.defense.gov/Transcripts/Transcript.aspx?TranscriptID=5619. Accessed on April 28, 2015.

GAO/T-NSIAD-99-196. (1999). *United Nations Observations on Reform Initiatives.* http://www.gao.gov/assets/110/107972.pdf. Accessed on October 17, 2017.

ISAB. (2015). *International Security Advisory Board Report on a Framework for International Cyber Stability.* http://www.state.gov/t/avc/isab/229023.htm. Accessed on April 28, 2015.

Jervis, Robert. (2010). Why Intelligence and Policymakers Clash. *Political Science Quarterly.* 125(2): 185–204.

Lamy, Steve L., John S. Masker, John Baylis, Steve Smith, and Patricia Owens. (2015). *Introduction to Global Politics.* Oxford University Press, Oxford, United Kingdom.

Lowenthal, Mark M. (2015). *Intelligence: From Secrets to Policy* (6th Edition). CQ Press.

Obama, Barack H. (2015). *Statement by the President on the Framework to Prevent Iran from Obtaining a Nuclear Weapon on April 2, 2015.* https://www.whitehouse.gov/the-press-office/2015/04/02/statement-president-framework-prevent-iran-obtaining-nuclear-weapon. Accessed on April 28, 2015.

Quinlan, Gary. (2014). *United Nations Security Council Letter from the Chair of United Nations Security Council Committee Pursuant to Resolutions 1267 and 1989.* http://www.un.org/en/ga/search/view_doc.asp?symbol=S/2014/815. Accessed on November 21, 2014.

Trump, Donald. (2017). *Remarks by President Trump to the 72nd Session of the United Nations.* https://www.whitehouse.gov/the-press-office/2017/09/19/remarks-president-trump-72nd-session-united-nations-general-assembly. Accessed on September 26, 2017.

Weaver, John M. (2016). Friend or Foe (or Do We Really Know)? Intelligence Community Contemporary Challenges (Chapter). In *Globalization: Economic, Political, and Social Issues.* Nova Science Publishers, New York [(Bernadette Gonzalez (editor)].

Weaver, John M. (Editor) with Jennifer Pomeroy (Editor). (2016). *Intelligence Analysis: Unclassified Area and Point Estimates (and Other Intelligence Related Topics).* Nova Science Publishers, New York.

Weaver, John M. (2018a). Dissecting the 2017 National Security Strategy: Implications for Senior Administrators (the Devil in the Details). *Global Policy.* 9(2): 283–284.

Weaver, John M. (2018b). The 2017 National Security Strategy of the United States. *Journal of Strategic Security.* 11(1): 62–71.

WEF. (2018). The Global Risks Report 2018 (13th Edition). *World Economic Forum.* http://www3.weforum.org/docs/WEF_GRR18_Report.pdf.

White House Briefing. (2015). *Press Briefing by the Press Secretary Josh Earnest on November 6, 2014.* https://www.whitehouse.gov/the-press-office/2014/11/06/press-briefing-press-secretary-josh-earnest-1162014. Accessed on April 28, 2015.

Wilcox, John. (2010). Rebalancing the Regional D.I.M.E. *Strategic Research Project, Army War College.* http://oai.dtic.mil/oai/oai?verb=getRecord&metadataPrefix=html&identifier=ADA522098. Accessed on November 25, 2014.

· 2 ·

RESEARCH QUESTIONS, METHODOLOGY, AND LIMITATIONS

Research Questions

This book posits that the five-permanent member (P5) nations of the United Nations Security Council either want to maintain or increase their stature in the world. Moreover, there are implications for the intelligence professionals throughout the globe in general and the men and women of the intelligence community of the U.S. more specifically. Understanding how the P5 members are either using or will use the variables of the York Intelligence Red Team Model—Modified will have an effect on how intelligence professionals should interpret information leading to the production of intelligence products. Their permanent presence on the Security Council has real and significant power regarding what the U.N. pursues in terms of actionable resolutions.

With the background established, the study will explore three research questions. Specifically, the author will look to answer "how," "why," and "what" questions regarding what is taking place in the context of the four other permanent members of the Security Council of the United Nations (the U.S. excluded) and what this means to the United States, its IC, and other intelligence personnel.

Q1: How are the permanent members of the Security Council of the United Nations using the instruments of national power to shape outcomes favorable to them?

Q2: Why are the permanent members of the Security Council of the United Nations using the instruments of national power to shape outcomes favorable to them?

Q3: What are the implications for the United States?

Methodology

Modern research has shown the viability of secondary data (Remler & Van Ryzin, 2010, p. 180). Secondary data types are low cost and often are quite accessible; researchers and practitioners alike in the policy and social science fields have turned to these sources to leverage this data for the purpose of conducting research (Remler & Van Ryzin, 2010, p. 180). This is particularly true even in the field of intelligence where professional analysts look to pull raw information from open sources of data.

Data used in this book came from secondary unclassified open sources solely. The study also consists of mostly secondary sources from the United States, but also takes into account those from international sources as well. More to the point, this author used qualitative techniques to triangulate on results (Remler & Van Ryzin, 2010). Creswell (2008) also provides an understanding of qualitative techniques. Specifically, he writes on the strength in using this methodology in exploration of relationships among variables in the quest to answer research questions (Creswell, 2008). This study looks at four small case studies with regards to the non-U.S. P5 member nations (China, France, Russia, and the U.K.).

Intelligence analysts are advised to seek out a variation of sources from as many collection disciplines as possible to help ensure a complete and comprehensive approach to problem dissection. Accordingly, this author made use of a model previously covered in other research to help balance his approach to problem dissection. The model used throughout this research is the Federal Qualitative Secondary Data Case Study Triangulation Model found in Figure 2.1 (Weaver, 2015).

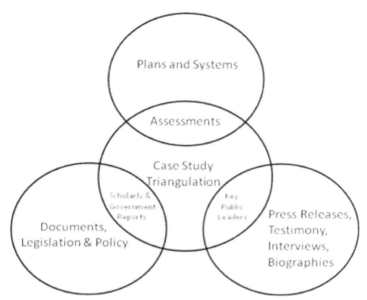

Figure 2.1. Federal Qualitative Secondary Data Case Study Triangulation Model.

The model is a Venn diagram and consists of three circular components. The first includes plans and systems as well as assessments of those plans and systems. The model also turns to a multitude of written works. These include government documents, legislation, scholarly reports and more; often these are seen as the most credible in the eyes of a majority of researchers. The final component takes on an oral feel; it turns to testimony, press statements coming from official government agencies, speeches, interviews, and information covered by key leaders.

To assist in compiling data, the author made use of meta-analysis techniques. One can find more specificity on key words (and their synonyms), search engines, and sites used for this study in Annex 2.1.

The author made used of a modification to a model called the York Intelligence Red Team Model (YIRTM) shown in Figure 2.2 to analyze data (Weaver & Pomeroy, 2016). The YIRTM is predicated on the four instruments of national power and includes diplomacy, information, military, and economic means (Weaver, 2016). The modified model (YIRTM-M) was used due to changing circumstances and model modification is acceptable according to Glassick (2000). Visually it represents the application of the instruments of national power on behalf of a government to shape outcomes and represents intervening relationships. Directionality along with temporal precedence can lend greater credence to the relevance of this logic model (Weaver & Pomeroy, 2016). This particular ordering of elements is a useful, but by no means could these specific variables be the only factors one considers for helping to establish an understanding of relationships of these instruments to shape outcomes. It includes all of the components except for the weakened U.S. position since this piece presumes that generally, the United Kingdom and France would like to see a strong United States.

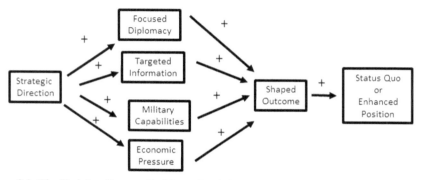

Figure 2.2. The York Intelligence Red Team Model—Modified (YIRTM-M).

The model begins with the strategic direction of the country and how it wants to ensure self-survival through guidance directed by its senior leadership. It provides basics on the "who," "what," "why," "when" and "where." Moreover, this strategic direction focuses the national security apparatus of that country to move towards understanding "who" should have primacy for "what" they are doing, and "when" things should be done to better understand "how" they would go about doing it and "why." The four instruments of power are a useful way to do this in order for the country to implement their TTPs supportive of one's cause.

Diplomacy is the first of instruments (Weaver & Pomeroy, 2016). Particularly, it involves leaders that engage others to bring about conditions favorable to what one wants to achieve regarding his or her country. It affords consideration not only to the application to one specific country but should also look regionally and/or globally at outcomes that decisions will have in surrounding countries and beyond.

Information is inherently linked to power and the selected use of it could thereby effectively influence activities throughout the globe. Targeted messaging quite often has merit to sway popular opinion to help promote one's cause; often this is done in simultaneity to delegitimize the messaging of another country or non-state actor. Likewise, adversaries use information through social media outlets as a way to inexpensively "educate" others to causes aligned to their interests to garner greater support as the country expands its position. Inextricably aligned to this instrument is the use of cyber. It is often seen as the least expensive of the instruments of power; it is readily available to all countries and non-state actors alike (Weaver, 2016).

Conventionally speaking, the military instrument is the most notable one known throughout the world (Weaver, 2016). This author looked at military capabilities of the four permanent members of the U.N. Security Council and their competence and vulnerabilities.

Money is a prerequisite to implement all actions of a government (Weaver & Pomeroy, 2016). It underpins most activities and has always been associated with power. Economically, nations can exert influence by using the power derived from money to coerce others to change behavior. Likewise, state actors can look for opportunities to weaken another's economy by exposing vulnerabilities and in the case of this study, at how to weaken those in opposition to its position in the world.

Validity is a concern with all scholarly research (Creswell, 2008). Accordingly, this piece addressed the topic of validity; it looked at two aspects. First, variable checks were used. These included efforts to ensure that variables measured what they were supposed to measure.

Secondly, face validity was considered to ensure that models and variables inherently made sense (Creswell, 2008). Likewise, face validity techniques evaluated the modified YIRTM model, variable directionality and its purpose to ensure that what was covered was not counterintuitive to what one reasonably considers when looking at shaped outcomes. Moreover, the Federal Qualitative Secondary Data Case Study Triangulation Model, which has been vetted and used in other studies, afforded this author the opportunity to ensure a balanced approach when considering data sources (Weaver, 2015, 2016).

The author looked at reliability. Consistency in research approaches considered similar projects to contribute to reliability (Creswell, 2008, p. 190). Likewise, Remler and Van Ryzin (2010, p. 118) have attested to the necessity of consistency in measurements while looking to achieve reliability in conducting research. Facilitation was fostered by the consistency of the D.I.M.E. as instruments of power and the use of the YIRTM-M and the Federal Qualitative Secondary Data Case Study Triangulation Model to analyze the data sources.

Limitations

As is the case with studies that focus solely on secondary data, research using this type of information is limited in such areas as the variables to explore and the temporal period considered. Generally, the scope of this research was limited to a five-year period from 2013 to March of 2018 though some instances dating beforehand were included. More weight was assigned to data in the latter years due to the relevance as it pertains to the future and because of the ever-evolving world situation in the context of a globalized market. Though the variables in the YIRTM-M were selected, other influencers exist that could impact the true value of each.

Only intervening relationships were considered. It is possible that other moderators could have an impact on the interpretation of results. These might include legacy trade agreements, treaties, sophistication of technology, and more. Forthcoming studies might consider these to build upon the results of this study.

Likewise, as is the case with all qualitative research, it is difficult to generalize beyond this study. The analysis of data and the results focus solely on the use of the variables in this study in particular as it applies to the specific actors mentioned in the study.

Other weaknesses from secondary data emanate from a cross-sectional design. Due to the reliance on secondary data, it is difficult for one to understand whether or not bias existed from how the data was originally collected (Cross-Sectional, 2012). Challenges can also arise regarding the cross-sectional process when interpreting results in part based on bias issues and the lack of full inclusion of all events (Cross-Sectional, 2012).

Primary sources were not considered and these include such techniques as personal observations, interviews and surveys. Though excluded, future studies might consider these techniques to either reconstruct the study or to complement its findings.

Provided that one understands that no research is a complete panacea, results can be useful. Moreover, as additional information becomes available, results from this study can be used in confirmatory research or in a contributory effort to help expand on efforts looking at the UNSC P5 members in the context of the YIRTM-M.

Annex 2.1: Meta-Analysis

Words	Words
Africa	Economy
Air Force	Espionage
Analysis	EU
Armed Forces	Europe
Army	European Union
Assessment	Evidence
Asia	FBI
Background	Federal Bureau of Investigation
Biography	Finance
Britain	France
Bureau	FSB
C2	G7
C4ISR	G8
China	G20
CNA	GCHQ
CND	GDP
CNE	Government
CNO	Government Report
CNR	Gross Domestic Product
Congress	GRU
Cyber	Hard Power
Cyberspace	History
Data	Human Intelligence
Defense	HUMINT
DGSE	IC
DGSI	Information
D.I.M.E.	Intelligence
Diplomacy	Intelligence Community
Diplomatic	Interviews
DRM	Iran
Economic	Islamic State

Words	*Words*
IS	PLAAF
ISIL	PLAN
ISIS	Plan
JCPOA	Plans
Joint Comprehensive Plan of Action	Policy
Joint Security Plan	Power
Journal	Premier
Judicial	Press Release
JSP	Reconnaissance
KGB	Report
Korea	Research
Leader	Russia
Legislation	Speech
Marine	Soft Power
MI5	Surveillance
MI6	Syria
Middle East	Testimony
Military	UK
Minister	United Kingdom
National Defense Strategy	UN
NATO	United Nations
Navy	United Nations Security Council
NDS	UNSC
NSA	SCS
NSS	Security
National Security Strategy	SIGINT
SIGINT	Signals Intelligence
OSD	South China Sea
P5	Supreme Court
Parliament	SVR
Permanent Members	System
PLA	Systems

Words	Websites/Key Word Search Sites
TECHINT	CRS.gov
Terror	C-Span.org
Terrorism	DHS.gov
TPP	DOD.mil
TTP	GAO.gov
Vulnerability	Google Scholar
Weapon Systems	House.gov
WEF	NATO.int
World Economic Forum	ODNI.gov
Worldwide Threat Assessment	NSA.gov
WTA	Senate.gov
	State.gov
Websites/Key Word Search Sites	UN.org
CIA.gov	Whitehouse.gov
CBO.gov	YCP Summons Search

References

Creswell, J.W. (2008). *Research Design; Qualitative, Quantitative, and Mixed Methods Approaches*. Thousand Oaks, CA: SAGE Publications.

Cross-Sectional. (2012). *Cross-Sectional Studies*. http://www.healthknowledge. org.uk/public-h ealth-textbook/research-methods/1a-epidemiology/cs-as-is/cross-sectional-studies. Accessed on October 17, 2012.

Glassick, Charles E. (2000). Boyer's Expanded Definitions of Scholarship, the Standards for Assessing Scholarship, and the Elusiveness of the Scholarship of Teaching. *Academic Medicine*. 75(9): 877–880.

Remler, D.K. and Van Ryzin, G.G. (2010). *Research Methods in Practice: Strategies for Description and Causation*. Thousand Oaks, CA: SAGE Publications.

Weaver, John M. (2015). The Perils of a Piecemeal Approach to Fighting ISIS in Iraq. *Public Administration Review*. 75(2): 192–193.

Weaver, John M. (2016). Friend or Foe (or Do We Really Know)? Intelligence Community Contemporary Challenges (Chapter). In *Globalization: Economic, Political, and Social Issues*. Nova Science Publishers [(Bernadette Gonzalez (editor)].

Weaver, John M. (Editor) with Jennifer Pomeroy (Editor). (2016). *Intelligence Analysis: Unclassified Area and Point Estimates (and Other Intelligence Related Topics)*. Nova Science Publishers, New York.

· 3 ·

UNITED NATIONS (CONTEXT)

History

The United Nations (U.N.) as an organization has existed since 1945; at present it is comprised of 193 member states (UN, 2018). It is headquartered in New York City, and has the ability to work on a myriad of issues that include peace and security, climate change, human rights, development, humanitarian crisis, health issues, disarmament, human rights, and terrorism (UN, 2018). This international organization helps foster cooperation among nations and works to help keep international order in the world (Roberts & Kingsbury, 1993). The U.N. affords member states an opportunity to express issues and concerns. They can do so vis-à-vis the General Assembly, the Security Council, its Economic and Social Council, as well as other committees and bodies (UN, 2018). The head of the U.N. is the Secretary General.

It officially came into existence on October 24th, 1945 after representatives from 50 of the countries throughout the world met in San Francisco. Its charter was signed months earlier in June of that same year (Lamy, Masker, Baylis, Smith, & Owens, 2015).

Throughout its 70-plus years of existence, it has served at the epicenter of many significant events. From inception and through the 1970s, it has been fraught with challenging, mostly stemming from the Cold War and the two protagonists during this period, the Soviet Union and the United States. In 1947, it approved the creation of the Israel as a nation (UN, 2018). Likewise, it authorized the U.S. and its partners to counter an attack by the Democratic People's Republic of Korea against its southern neighbor (UN, 2018). The U.N. also formed a peace keeping force to help resolve the crisis in the Suez Canal in 1956 (UN, 2018).

Moving into the 1960s, it deployed personnel to the Congo to help resolve the conflict on the African continent (UN, 2018). It also helped with garnering support to peacekeeping operations in Cypress (UN, 2018). As France and the United Kingdom released control of their former colonies, new nations joined the U.N. and the organization began to grow.

As the Cold War waned, the U.N. was there to assist with peace keeping operations (Pugh, 2001). The United Nations backed a call for military action supporting the U.S. coalition to ouster the Iraqis after they took over Kuwait in 1990. These also included support to operations in Somalia, Haiti, and Bosnia in the early-to-mid 1990s (UN, 2018).

The Organs

The organization has a formal structure consisting of six organs. These include the General Assembly, Security Council, Economic and Social Council, Trusteeship Council, International Court of Justice, and the Secretariat (Lamy et al., 2015).

The General Assembly is the key organ responsible for deliberations and policy making. Annually in the month of September, member states meet and many heads of state address the assembly. Votes generally require approval from a simple majority; the exceptions pertain to new member admission, issues regarding peace and security, as well as budgetary matters (UN, 2018).

The Economic and Social Council is the proponent responsible to the U.N. for coordination, review of policy, providing recommendations on economic, environmental, and social issues; it also looks to implement goals that are agreed to internationally (Lamy et al., 2015).

Third, the Trusteeship Council had wielded power for years. Its mission was complete in May of 1994 when all Trust Territories obtained independence or self-governance (UN, 2018).

The International Court of Justice is the judicial organ of the United Nations and is the only one not headquartered in New York. It is located in The Hague in The Netherlands and its expressed mission is to help settle legal disputes by nations in accordance with international law (Lamy et al., 2015).

The Secretariat has the responsibility for administrative functions. It oversees U.N. employees who perform the daily work required to help run the organization (Lamy et al., 2015). The Secretary General overseas the organization and is appointed by the General Assembly based on the recommendation from the Security Council.

Finally, the Security Council is charged with the maintenance of international peace and security (Lamy et al., 2015). It consists of five permanent and 10 rotational members. The permanent members include China, France, Russia, the United Kingdom, and the United States. Each member is afforded with one vote and under the charter, all member states must comply with Security Council decisions. Its power is also derived from the ability of this council to leverage sanctions against nations and even authorize the use of force against a country (Lamy et al., 2015). Each of the permanent members has the power to veto a decision and if so, it only takes one to stop an action from proceeding.

References

Lamy, Steven, John Masker, John Baylis, Steve Smith, and Patricia Owens. (2015). *Introduction to Global Politics* (3rd Edition). Oxford University Press, Oxford, UK.

Pugh, M. (2001). Peacekeeping and Humanitarian Intervention. In *Issues in World Politics* (2nd Edition). Palgrave, London.

Roberts, A. and Kingsbury, B. (1993). Introduction: The UN's Roles in International Society Since 1945. In *United Nations, Divided World*. Oxford, UK.

UN. (2018). *United Nations*. http://www.un.org/en/index.html. Accessed on April 18, 2018.

· 4 ·

THE UNITED STATES
(AN OVERVIEW OF PRIORITIES)

President Trump released his National Security Strategy (NSS) in late December of 2017. It is the quintessential source serving as the azimuth for key government leaders to guide them through the execution of core functions at federal departments and agencies in the months and years to come (Weaver, 2018a). It is only 55 pages long; it outlines the nexus of issues that he and by extension, his National Security Council, see as of paramount concern for the United States. Broadly, Trump looks to (1) protect the homeland, (2) promote the prosperity of the U.S., (3) leveraging strength in order to preserve peace, and (4) advance U.S. influence throughout the world (NSS, 2017, p. 4). Likewise, the National Defense Strategy and U.S. Department of State's Joint Strategic Plan came out in early 2018.

The Homeland

The president identified early on key threats to the United States and these include among a multitude of issues, North Korea and its pursuit of weapons of mass destruction capable of reaching the United States (Wright, 2009, p. 5). Others include Iran's support of terrorist groups, jihadist terror organizations whose ideology is targeting the American people, and threats from cyber (NSS, 2017, p. 7).

Moreover, the NSS addresses a series of priority risks and these include national security, energy, finance and banking, safety and health, communications, and transportation (NSS, 2017, p. 13). The U.S. accordingly should invest in infrastructure protection and hardening of key targets to make them less susceptible to physical attacks especially ports (air and sea), railways and roads, the telecommunications industry, as well as transit systems (NSS, 2017, p. 19). Other measures identified include sealing off porous entry points into the United States; these include the creation of a wall and vetting those seeking entry to the United States (NSS, 2017, p. 10). The Joint Strategic Plan of the U.S. Department of State also underscores the importance of security at home through its Joint Strategic Plan or JSP (JSP, 2018, p. 23). The Defense Department plan underscores that though the homeland is not a sanctuary for terror organizations, America is still a target with exposed vulnerabilities in the areas of cyber threats, possible future attacks on its citizens, and more (NDS, 2018, p. 3). The federal government will also be critical in working with state and local governments to identify cyber threats and to help ensure resiliency of networks to exposure from state and non-state nefarious types alike especially for communications networks, the financial and banking sector, transportation, and the health sector. The United States sees threats in terms of cyber hackers, malevolent non-state actors, and more (NDS, 2018, p. 3).

The U.S. will have to promote strong diplomatic relations with China, South Korea, and Japan to show regional resolve regarding North Korea to help protect its homeland and will also be instrumental in garnering support among the four other permanent members of the United Nations Security Council in seeking to castigate Kim Jong-un's regime (Weaver, 2018b, p. 65). It will be involved in implementing a comprehensive missile defense system and will be called to pursue transnational terrorism threats at their source (NSS, 2017, pp. 8–10). It will also be critical to work with state and local governments to identify cyber threats and to help ensure resiliency of networks to exposure from the likes of state and non-state nefarious types and to share information with key allies (and by extension, their intelligence services) throughout the world (NSS, 2017, p. 13).

Prosperity

The U.S. will have significant challenges regarding the promotion of American prosperity. It will be necessary to pursue negotiating trade agreements more favorable to the United States; this comes at a period when U.S. growth has been averaging only 2% over recent years compared to China's double-digit numbers. Likewise, it will want to keep sea lanes open to foster free trade especially in the South China Sea where China has asserted greater influence in recent years. The National Defense Strategy also shows that China is engaged in predatory economics and other influence operations with the expressed intent of bolstering its prosperity (NDS, 2018, p. 2).

Peace Through Strength Abroad

The president has underscored what he calls preserving peace through strength showing the U.S. as still being a relevant global actor (NSS, 2017, p. 23). In doing so, he identifies China and Russia as major challengers to the United States (NSS, 2017, p. 2). The U.S. will also turn to diplomacy to strengthen relations and alliances in Europe and Asia (for military basing rights, trade, and more) while looking to engage both countries to find common interests in order to help turn around the deterioration in the state of affairs seen in recent years regarding both. The U.S. will most likely continue military exchanges and participation in show of force exercises to demonstrate U.S. capabilities and resolve.

Trump has concerns for Iran's sponsorship of terror organizations and the possibility that it might renege on its agreement to halt uranium enrichment (NSS, 2017, p. 26). Accordingly, it must lean on the United Nations and the International Atomic Energy Agency to keep pressure on Iran to compel it to move away from terror support and from going back to pursuing a nuclear weapons' development program especially as the U.S. has pulled out of the nuclear agreement and as it possibly looks to renegotiate terms. The Defense Department of the United States sees Iran as an actor that has intentions of becoming a regional power and also sees it as a state sponsor of terrorism in the Middle East (NDS, 2018, p. 2).

The NSS (2017) further states that North Korea has invested heavily in a ballistic missile program and has developed a significant nuclear capability. The Defense Department has even gone as far to consider North Korea as a rogue regime bent on destabilizing the region of Northeast Asia (NDS, 2018, p. 2). Even the Department of State is fully behind the idea of countering the proliferation of weapons of mass destruction to include from this regime (JSP, 2018, p. 23). Aside from what was covered about this rouge regime in the Homeland section of the NSS, the U.S. will have a role regionally in maintaining a formidable forward military presence in South Korea, Japan, and Guam and through the provision of missile defense capabilities in Northeast Asia. This shows both resolve and commitment to U.S. allies.

Jihadist operating throughout the world is another major concern. As Trump, and by extension his federal departments and agencies, look to implement the NSS, he needs to figure out how the U.S. will apply economic pressure to cut off funding, look to use the military kinetically to take out terror command and control centers of gravity, and turn to the State Department to leverage capabilities (diplomatic, military and economic) of friends and allies to collectively prosecute targeting while simultaneously looking to help defeat the ideology through a successful campaign using information dispelling the falsehoods of their messaging. What's more is that the State Department's JSP looks to leverage partnerships to defeat the Islamic State, al-Qaeda and other terror organizations the world over (JSP, 2018, p. 25). Likewise, it can selectively distribute aid and support efforts to prevent countries from digressing to weak or failed states that could harbor transnational jihadists particularly by supporting governments that are allied with the United States.

Advancing American Influence

The United States looks to keep its relevancy as a hegemonic power. Accordingly, it would like to counter emerging powers like China and Russia as they look to wrest influence and power from this nation. Likewise, the U.S. wants to reduce dependency of other nations on this nation's foreign aid (NSS, 2017, p. 39). The NSS also sees the importance of leveraging the Department of State in crafting trade agreements with countries in Africa, Asia, and Latin America (NSS, 2017, p. 39). The U.S. also plans to use technology to serve in a complementary role to diplomatic efforts abroad and would like to support incentivizing reforms across the globe to include such organizations like the International Monetary Fund, Work Bank, and World Trade Organization (NSS, 2017, p. 40). Though it is important for the U.S. to remain the global leader (through the United States' vision), it desires holding other countries accountable and to have them share the financial burden when solving complex problems.

The United States has begun a reinvestment in its military as a way to reverse the atrophy of power in recent years (NDS, 2018, p. 1). It is doing so to stem the erosion of influence it has seen in recent years in order to be able to project influence worldwide to deter war and protect vital security interests of the country (NDS, 2018).

Soft Power

The U.S. State Department is committed to helping bring the NSS to fruition. To help realize this, it will execute its plan through four primary goals.

The first is to protect the U.S. security at home and abroad (JSP, 2018, p. 23). To better achieve this, it will pursue strategic objectives. The first sub goal involves efforts to counter weapons of mass destruction proliferation (JSP, 2018, p. 23). The department will actively employ diplomatic engagement in order to leverage partner nations' strengths (JSP, 2018, p. 25). Likewise it will work with sister departments from within the federal government to achieve synergy through such organizations like the Department of Energy, Department of Justice, Department of Treasury, and Department of Commerce.

It hopes to also defeat terror organizations like the Islamic State and al-Qaeda under another sub goal (JSP, 2018, p. 24). Similar to goal 1.1, it intends to do this through working with U.S. federal departments and agencies at home while also seeking out assistance diplomatically from other countries' defense, law enforcement, and judicial sectors (JSP, 2018, p. 26). It also will serve in a complementary capacity to the other major department involved in foreign engagement, the Department of Defense (JSP, 2018, p. 27).

Soft power initiatives under goal one also looks through countering transnational crime and violence directed at U.S. interests (JSP, 2018, p. 27). It hopes to realize success through strengthened citizen-responsive governance, supporting democracy globally, fostering human rights, and promoting security initiatives (JSP, 2018, p. 29).

Under the goal of protecting America's security, it looks at two additional sub goals. These include strengthening resiliency of partners and allies and improving boarder security at home.

The JSP covers a second goal: renewing the competitive advantage for America pertaining to economic growth (JSP, 2018, p. 23). Under this heading, a sub goal of the department is looking to leverage international organizations and bilateral agreements that will result in commercial arrangements to help improve its economic position (JSP, 2018 p. 23). What's more is that the State Department is interested in open markets and the pursuit of initiatives that will lead to economic security and reforms in the areas of governance and economic initiatives.

Soft power initiatives continue. The JSP then turns to its third major goal of promoting leadership in the world through balanced engagement (JSP, 2018). To achieve this, the department wants to pull back from aid distribution while it looks to foster the continuance of partnership the world over. It will remain engaged through foreign policy initiatives that strive to balance the burden of world leadership with other nations simpatico with the values espoused by the United States (JSP, 2018).

Hard Power

The Defense Department is poised to leverage the military instrument of power if and when needed. Moreover, it is committed to defending the homeland from attack (NDS, 2018, p. 4). This will include an investment in a ballistic missile defense system, employment of National Guard personnel along the southern border of the United States, and the construction of a wall.

This department will utilize technological superiority of weapon systems and employ forces as necessary globally and specifically in key regions (NDS, 2018, p. 4). The intention here will be to employ stand-off measures to minimize troop exposure where possible to threats from state and non-state actors alike. In doing so, it hopes to deter adversarial aggression that could be directed against national security interests.

More specifically, the arraying of U.S. forces will occur throughout the Indo-Pacific, on the European continent, the continuance of operations in the Middle East, and the security of the Western Hemisphere (NDS, 2018). Inextricably linked to this is the desire to defend key allies from military aggression from nefarious actors (NDS, 2018).

Prevention of hostilities is preferred to reacting to acts of violence. Accordingly, DOD is committed to prevent terrorists from realizing success both at home and abroad (NDS, 2018). Along the line of terror, will include serving as a force to dissuade, prevent, and deter state and non-state actors from pursing the acquisition and use of weapons of mass destruction (NDS, 2018).

To realize success, the Defense Department will apply a strategic approach. This includes the use of the four known instruments of power and the understanding of the following: finance, intelligence, and law enforcement (NDS, 2018, p. 4). Likewise, it will invest in military modernization initiatives. These include the likes of the nuclear triad (nuclear missiles, sub launched ballistic missiles, and nuclear bombs capable of being dropped from aircraft).

Investments will also include space and cyberspace capabilities to operate in a myriad of domains (NDS, 2018). Other efforts will result in enhancements to C4ISR (command, control, communications, computer, intelligence, surveillance, and reconnaissance) systems. These C4ISR systems will also help improve joint lethality, and to help the force maneuver more effectively and to help ensure resiliency to threats and redundancy so as to not have one severed link end with a catastrophic impact on mission execution.

Finally, as DOD works to support the NSS, its sees value in partnerships (NDS, 2018). It will integrate with interagency partners at home and hopes to leverage coalitions like NATO (NDS, 2018, p. 5).

The next four chapters look at what is taking place regarding China, France, Russia, and the United Kingdom. Moreover they cover what is occurring in the context of the modified YIRTM-M with data sources focused on those covered in the Federal Secondary Data Case Study Triangulation Model while looking at the U.N. in general.

References

JSP. (2018). *Joint Strategic Plan FY 2018–2022 U.S. Department of State and U.S. Agency for International Development.* https://www.state.gov/documents/organization/277156.pdf. Accessed on April 17, 2018.

NDS. (2018). *National Defense Strategy.* https://www.defense.gov/Portals/1/Documents/pubs/2018-National-Defense-Strategy-Summary.pdf. Accessed on January 20, 2018.

NSS. (2017). *National Security Strategy of the United States of America.* http://nssarchive.us/wp-content/uploads/2017/12/2017.pdf. Accessed on December 23, 2017.

Weaver, John M. (2018a). Dissecting the 2017 National Security Strategy: Implications for Senior Administrators (the Devil in the Details). *Global Policy.* 9(2): 283–284.

Weaver, John M. (2018b). The 2017 National Security Strategy of the United States. *Journal of Strategic Security.* 11(1): 62–71.

Wright, David. (2009). *North Korea's Missile Program.* https://www.ucsusa.org/sites/default/files/legacy/assets/documents/nwgs/north-koreas-missile-program.pdf. Accessed on January 10, 2018.

· 5 ·

CHINA

History and Background of China

China, for centuries has been a leading civilization often outperforming the rest of the world in both the arts and sciences. However as it moved into the 19th and early 20th centuries, it succumbed to major famines, civil unrest, military defeats, and even foreign occupation (CIA, 2018). Following World War II, Mao Zedong, along with China's communist party established an autocratic socialist system that led to the imposition of strict controls over daily life and resulted in the lost lives of tens of millions of people. Focus shifted to market-oriented economic development after 1978 (under the leadership of Deng Ziaoping) and by 2000 its economic output had increased by a factor of four (CIA, 2018). The standard of living has improved dramatically since, but political controls remain tight. Since the early 1990s, China has increased its global outreach and has becoming increasingly involved in becoming a prominent force in international organizations (Gries, 2004).

Presently, China remains a communist country and pursues economic initiatives under the notion of state sponsored capitalism. The government consists of an executive branch where the chief of state is President Xi Jinping and the head of government falls to Premier Li Kequiang (CIA, 2018). The country's president and vice president are elected (indirectly) by the National People's Congress for five year terms.

China has a robust military (Hu, 2011). Its primary ground component is referred to as the People's Liberation Army (PLA). China's maritime components consist of its navy (PLAN) and include marines and naval aviation forces (CIA, 2018). The air component, the air force (known as the Zhongguo Renmin Jiefangjun Kongjun or PLAAF) includes airborne forces, a rocket force (strategic missile force), and a strategic support force (which encompasses space and cyber forces) (CIA, 2018). The People's Armed Police (called the Renmin Wuzhuang Jingcha Budui or PAP) provides for internal security and finally, the PLA Reserve Force rounds out the country's military (CIA, 2018).

China has a legislative branch referred to as Quanguo Renmin Daibiao Dahui. It consists of 2,987 seats whereby its membership is indirectly elected by various people's congresses (by municipality, region, or province) (CIA, 2018). Similar to the president and vice president, legislative members are elected for a five-year term (Gries, 2004).

The judicial branch oversees the legal affairs of the country (Gries, 2004). Its highest court is the Supreme People's Court which is comprised of 340 judges and includes a chief justice and 13 grand justices that are further structured under tribunals and a civil committee for economic, civil, administrative, communications and transportation, complaints and appeals cases (CIA, 2018). Judges are appointed by the People's National Congress and are limited to two consecutive five year terms (CIA, 2018). China also has a subordinate judicial court structure that includes the Higher People's Courts, District and County People's Courts, Autonomous Region People's Courts, and Special People's Courts for maritime, military, transportation, and issues pertaining to forestry (CIA, 2018).

China in recent decades has moved from a centrally planned and closed system to a more market-oriented economy that plays a major global role (Gries, 2004). This country has implemented reforms incrementally and what has resulted has been an increase in efficiency gains that have contributed to a more than tenfold increase in its gross domestic product (CIA, 2018). The country is persistent in its "going global" strategy and is constantly looking to pave a path forward towards economic development and growth (Li, 2010, p. 235). China continues to pursue an industrial policy that is underpinned by state support of key sectors. In 2016, China stood as the largest economy in the world, surpassing the U.S. in 2014 for the first time in modern history

(CIA, 2018). Dating back to 2010, China became the world's largest exporter and subsequently became the largest trading nation in 2013 (CIA, 2018). What is surprising is that China's per capita income is below the world average.

China for years has kept is currency closely linked to the U.S. dollar. However, in July 2005, China moved to an exchange rate system that references a more heterogeneous mix of currencies (CIA, 2018). In later years (2013 until early 2015), the renminbi (RMB) appreciated by nearly 2% against the dollar; yet the exchange rate fell 13% from mid-2015 until the end of the calendar year of 2016 amid the external streaming in part stemming from the devaluation of China's currency in August 2015 (CIA, 2018). The RMB has bounced back and has gained value against the dollar by close to 7% from the end of 2016 to December of 2017 (CIA, 2018). From 2013 to 2017, China had one of the fastest growing economies in the world during this five-year period (Gries, 2004).

Yet, the Chinese Government faces several economic challenges including: (1) reducing its high domestic savings rate as compared to its low domestic household consumption; (2) its ability to effectively manage its high corporate debt burden to allow China to maintain financial stability; (3) controlling local government debt (not on the balance sheet) used to finance infrastructure stimulus; (4) facilitating job opportunities for the aspiring middle class that would foster greater wages and includes the likes of college graduates, and rural migrants while also maintaining its competitive edge; (5) temping down the real estate sector's speculative investment without adversely affecting the economy; (6) bringing down industrial overcapacity; and (7) pursing more efficient allocation of capital and state-support for innovation that would raise productivity growth rates (CIA, 2018).

What has resulted is the economic development that has progressed further in coastal provinces than in the country's interior. China is also seeing one of the rapidly aging populations on the planet and has since relaxed its "one-child policy" (Goldman, 2005). An environmental problem confronting China is a deterioration in air quality, the steady fall of the water table, soil, and erosion. What has resulted led China to seek alternate energy sources and capacity as it looks to move away from fossil fuel dependency (CIA, 2018). China has since ratified the Paris Agreement, and sees the viability of a multilateral agreement to combat climate change (CIA, 2018).

China is involved in transnational issues (Hu, 2011). Also, China has experienced issues with regional neighbors. It is involved in dialog and confidence-building initiatives to work toward reducing tensions over Kashmir (CIA, 2018). Nonetheless, the region remains militarized with portions under a triad of actors: Chinese administration (Aksai Chin), Pakistan (Azad Kashmir and Northern Areas) and India (Jammu and Kashmir). What is noteworthy is that India still fails to recognize Pakistan's ceding historic Kashmir lands to China in 1964 (CIA, 2018). Moreover, China and India continue their foreign policy and security talks that began in 2005 related to the dispute over most of their militarized boundary, issues pertaining to regional nuclear proliferation, and other nation state matters (CIA, 2018). Additionally, China has laid claim to the Arunachal Pradesh (which India has stated that it controls) to the base of the Himalayas (CIA, 2018). Due to a lack of treaty describing the formal boundary, Bhutan and China continue their negotiations to establish a common borderline to resolve territorial disputes that have arisen from substantial cartographic discrepancies (CIA, 2018).

Transnational issues continue with maritime disputes (Hu, 2011). Chinese version of maps shows that its international boundary extends off the coasts of the littoral states of the South China Seas, where it has been an impediment to hydrocarbon exploration by the Vietnamese (CIA, 2018). Chinese assertion include its sovereignty over the Scarborough Reef (a reef also claimed by the Philippines and Taiwan), and over the Spratly Islands (islands also claimed by Malaysia, the Philippines, Taiwan, Vietnam, and Brunei). China's maritime forays have led it to occupy some of the Paracel Islands (that are also claimed by Taiwan and Vietnam) (CIA, 2018). The Senkaku Islands, administered by Japan, are also claimed by China and Taiwan (CIA, 2018). China also has disputes with North Korea regarding islands in the Yalu and Tumen Rivers (CIA, 2018). Russia and China have also demarcated the islands at the Ussuri and Amuri confluence and in the Argun River (CIA, 2018).

Chinese Intelligence

China has an extensive intelligence structure seemingly adept at conducting both espionage and cyber activity (Lowenthal, 2017, p. 499). According to Lowenthal (2017, p. 499) it has two primary purposes: (1) to direct activities against dissidents (for internal security) and (2) to conduct foreign intelligence operations. The conduct of intelligence operations falls under the purview of the Ministry of State Security though it is dwarfed by the power possessed by its Central Military Commission (Lowenthal, 2017).

According to Lowenthal (2017), China's intelligence operations fall under 11 bureaus. The First Bureau centers efforts on Secret Intelligence collection; this organization focuses on the countries in both Europe and Central Asia (Lowenthal, 2017).

Its Second Bureau deals with open source intelligence collection (Lowenthal, 2017). It pulls data from overseas reporting sources and subsequently conducts analysis to complement intelligence gathered from other classified methods of collection.

China' Third and Fourth Bureaus look to gather information on Chinese unique interests. Specifically, they exist to gather information on both Hong Kong & Macau, and Taiwan respectively (Lowenthal, 2017).

The Fifth, Eighth, and Sixteenth Bureaus look more to phases and collection methodologies used by intelligence. The Fifth Bureau looks at analysis and evaluation stemming from data pulled from various sources of raw intelligence to interpret what is occurring (Lowenthal, 2017). China's Eighth Bureau focuses on denying foreign intelligence services access to sensitive information and state secrets by providing the country with counterintelligence support (Lowenthal, 2017). Finally, the Sixteenth Bureau provides the Ministry of State Security with imagery (Lowenthal, 2017).

Rounding out China's intelligence services include four additional bureaus. The Ninth Bureau provides technical support, security of government and party leaders is provided by the Tenth, the Eleventh focuses on international relations, and finally the Eighteenth Bureau turns its collection efforts to the United States (Lowenthal, 2017).

Analysis of China

China has emerged as a significant global actor on the world stage in recent years (Jalalzai, 2016, p. 18). According to the United Nations, it is the largest in terms of population in the world with an estimated count of 1.3 billion people (UN, 2014). When looking at the Gross Domestic Product (GDP), this nation ranks second only to the United States with a GDP value of approximately $11.2 trillion according to the International Monetary Fund (IMF, 2017). The latest edition of the United States' National Defense Strategy looks at China as a strategic competitor of this nation bent on using intimidation with regards to other nations in Asia while also militarizing the South China Sea (NDS, 2018, p. 1).

The rest of this section is dedicated to the application of the YIRTM-M and how it applies to China. Supporting data for this section is found in Annex 5.1. Here one will find the exact breakdown by instruments for the data supporting the analysis section. Likewise, the variation of sources tied back to the Federal Secondary Data Case Study Triangulation Model will also show the balance in sources contributing to the analysis of each instrument of national power.

Diplomatically, China has pushed to convince the world that its intentions both regionally and globally are benign (Crosston, 2016, p. 120). Much of what it has done underscores its desire to emphasize sovereignty and ostensibly coming across as nonchalant through its contemporary philosophy and cultural leanings (Crosston, 2016, p. 120). It has been using its influence through carrots and sticks to shape outcomes. Though China has been a vehement supporter of North Korea, it does see nuclear weapons on the peninsula as a destabilizing factor in the region. Accordingly, China supported most of the measures requested by the United States in response to North Korea's September 2017 nuclear tests thereby supporting to U.N. Security Council resolution 2375, tightening the pressure on North Korea (UN 2375, 2017).

President Xi Jinping met privately with President Trump at the G20 conference in early July, 2017. During this conference both leaders expressed an interest to enhance their economic positions regarding trade and market access (White House Press Release 1, 2017).

China's State Councilor, Yang Jiechi and the People's Liberation Army (PLA) Chief of Joint Staff, Fang Fenghui met with the U.S. Secretaries of State and Defense, Rex Tillerson and Jim Mattis respectively in late June 2017 (Joint Press Release, 2017). During the press conference, Tillerson and Mattis spoke of the next 40 years with Tillerson expressing concerns about anything that would tip the balance regarding the status quo in the region (Joint Press Release, 2017). During this conference Mattis went farther by acknowledging that competition between the nations was bound to occur and stressed the importance to avoid conflict particularly in the South China Sea (SCS) (Joint Press Release, 2017). What is somewhat reassuring is the inextricable linkage of the economies of both China and the United States at least for the foreseeable future (WEF, 2018, p. 36).

China is proficiently using cyber and information warfare globally (Rogers, 2017). The 2017 Worldwide Threat Assessment by the U.S. Director of National Intelligence sees China as an actor adept at using this TTP and will continue to do so to target governments of the U.S. and its allies and U.S. businesses (WTA, 2017, p. 1). In a speech to The New America Foundation in February of 2017, when discussion ensued with Admiral Rogers who headed the National Security Agency (NSA), a statement was made that China was a frequent culprit in stealing secrets vis-à-vis cyber (both private and government) from the United States. Moreover, it has invested in the capabilities to foster computer network operations (CNO) which more broadly includes computer network exploitation (CNE), and computer network attacks (CNA) in order to expose vulnerabilities in developed nations (Weaver, 2017a). It has most likely done so to target the United Nations, governments, corporations, and more for the purposes of gaining advantages both economically and militarily (Rudner, 2013, p. 454). Yet China is greatly concerned about its own cyber network defense (CND) to protect itself from exploitation by others that might engage in similar behavior.

China's intelligence apparatus is focused predominately on internal operations but it is becoming increasingly concerned with regional and global considerations (Crosston, 2016, p. 118). It is doing so to achieve the survival of its existence (Crosston, 2016, p. 119). Moreover, evidence from secondary sources point to China in particular as being adept at using cyber espionage as a way to infiltrate into government and private sector networks throughout the United States (Weaver, 2017). An assessment of China's People's Liberation Army capabilities also shows the relevancy of this country's acquisition of systems and capabilities to be used for cyber-attacks (Regional Focus, 2015).

In mid-May 2017, the U.S. Defense Department made public its annual report on China and its military. In this document, it intoned that China's leaders are bent on military modernization and the importance thereof for the pursuit of President Xi's "China Dream" for the rejuvenation of the nation (OSD, 2017, p. i). During the last year, its military budget grew by 8.5% with the intent to develop capacity to defeat adversaries and counter third party intervention efforts (to include the United States) (OSD, 2017, p. ii). To do this, it intends to invest in the acquisition of advanced weapon systems and technologies (OSD, 2017, p. 17). What's more, it has implemented research plans to improve aeronautic, information technologies, and nanotechnology (OSD, 2017, p. 70). Likewise, this country has robust military capabilities and is pursuing out-of-area operations as a way to demonstrate its strength to the world (Weaver, 2017).

Militarily, there are tensions in the SCS (GAO 17–369, 2017, p. 1). This has been spawned by China exerting greater influence in the region in recent years. In December of 2016, according to a DOD press release, a U.S unmanned underwater vehicle (UUV) was seized by China in the SCS while a U.S. Navy oceanographic survey ship was in the process of recovering it (P.R. 448-16, 2016).

All of this has come to fruition as China has increased its focus on building and modernizing its military (Crosston, 2016, p. 119). It is leveraging this instrument to influence activities in its region (NDS, 2018, p. 2). Likewise, it has done so to enhance its own border security while exerting greater maritime influences in the region (Crosston, 2016, p. 119). Of notable importance has been the rising military tension on its border between the two Koreas in recent years (Crosston, 2016, p. 119).

Economically, China has been engaged in cyber espionage to compress the research and development timeline to enhance its position in the world while improving its military capabilities (Weaver, 2017). Moreover, it will likely look to sustainability development and internal consumption over dependence on other nation states (Crosston, 2016, p. 121). China is also interested in enhancing its information technology sector as a way to grow market share in the world in this specific industry (WTA, 2017, p. 4).

China is also looking to expand influence throughout Asia, branching westward towards Europe, and even to Africa. It has done so through the China Belt and Road Initiative (BRI) dating back to 2013 which encompasses 60 counties and also includes the Pakistan Economic Corridor, and the Bangladesh-China-India-Myanmar Economic Corridor (WEF, 2018, p. 40). China is looking to develop relationships with Iran and Sudan as well (Li, 2010, p. 240).

Yet, this comes at a time when China is looking to maintain state influence over merchants in China (Li, 2010, p. 237). This has occurred in the backdrop of setbacks to liberalization and the press/media sectors (Li, 2010). Moreover, seven industries still remain under the control of the state—telecommunication, petroleum, defense, coal mining, electricity, civil aviation, and ocean shipping (Li, 2010).

Implications for Intelligence Professionals

As established earlier in this chapter, China is probably viewed as the primary contender as the nation most likely to threaten the position of the United States as the world's sole remaining hegemony; more specifically, it appears to be quite skilled at using diplomacy as a way to enhance its status. Intelligence professionals both in the United States and throughout the world should continue to monitor China's diplomatic ties. It appears to be investing in relationships that could have reverberations both militarily and economically. With the U.S. no longer as vested in the TPP initiative as it was under President Obama, China could potentially fill the leadership vacuum left by the U.S. pullout. When looking at China through the lens of the United Nations Security Council, it will support initiatives that would result in a balanced approach to limiting threats but only insofar as that they will not further the causes championed by the United States at the potential weakening of Chinese influence. It will most likely continue to use its 1st, 3rd, 10th, and 11th Bureaus under the Ministry of State Security to collect information on dissidents that it sees as a threat to China's sovereignty.

From an informational perspective, intelligence community (IC) professionals the world over should be weary of Chinese cyber influences in particular with its ability to conduct both CNA and CNE under the broader banner of CNO. Under the Ministry of State Security, China will make use of its 2nd and 9th Bureaus to collect information. China realizes that at present, it doesn't have the acumen of those working in the technical sector of the United States and for the foreseeable future will likely look for ways to acquire leading edge products and systems to compress the timeline from research and development to full up production of such things and intelligence-based systems and weapons. Likewise, China is investing in developing its own workforce which is in part why it sees value in western education venues by sending its students to study abroad at U.S. colleges and universities (and those in Europe as well). It will likely also invest in CND efforts to protect its own proprietary information and to mitigate network exploitation efforts from the United States and other nations if relations with other countries would falter. Though China sees the threat from cyber vulnerabilities, it will most likely avoid any U.N. resolutions limiting the use of cyber against other nations mostly because it stands to gain much from using cyber TTPs.

It is apparent that China is making a transition through its investment in its military. China's 5th and 16th Bureaus will assist China in gathering intelligence on military targets (particularly those of the United States. Intelligence professionals should look to see if they are continuing to strike a balance among all of its branches of the armed forces or if they are pursing counter efforts to U.S. technical platforms like U.S. stealth aircraft and naval vessels (with a particular focus on aircraft carriers). Likewise it will it look to continue the military buildup in the Spratly Islands to exert influence within the South China Sea. What's more, it will be interesting to see if diplomatic relations with other countries result in potential military basing rights for the country in the years to come drawing from the U.S. playbook of forward basing. When turning inward to defense, China will avoid U.N. resolutions that would result in anything that would stymie its military expansion to include maritime rights in the South China Sea.

Economically, the U.S. IC members and intelligence professionals from other countries should watch to see whether or not China will fill the void by fostering a multilateral trade agreement to replace the TPP. China's 2nd and 18th Bureaus will assist China in economic espionage. This could benefit China economically while putting the United States on defensive footing (and increasing the bureaucratic burden for the U.S. in trying to negotiate bilateral trade agreements). Moreover, the IC professionals throughout the world should look to see just how assertive China will become to "control" access to and through the South China Sea. The economic impact is not limited to the maritime sector. Ground lines of communication are affected through the China Belt and Road Initiative and IC personnel should look to see what other derivative benefits that China can realize through investment in this major undertaking and how this can challenge the United States and other nations as well. China's support of UNSC resolutions will always be viewed through the context of what this means for the country and how it can impact the growth of its GDP.

Annex 5.1 *China*

How/Why	D.I.M.E.	Author(s)	Source Type	Date	Page
China exerting influence in SCS	D, M	Joint Press Release	Press Release	2017	NA
Xi Jinping/Trump meet to discuss trade at G20	E	White House Press Release 1	Press Release	2017	NA
Military Modernization	M	OSD	Document	2017	i
Defeat adversaries and countering third party intervention	M	OSD	Document	2017	ii
Pursue advanced weapon systems and technologies	M	OSD	Document, China's Plans and Systems	2017	17

How/Why	D.I.M.E.	Author(s)	Source Type	Date	Page
Improve aeronautic, information technologies and nanotechnology	I, M	OSD	Document, China's Plans and Systems	2017	70
Militarily, there are tensions in the South China Sea	M	GAO 17-369	Government Document	2017	1
China was a frequent culprit in stealing secrets vis-à-vis cyber (both private and government)	I, E	Rogers	Speech	2017	NA
Target the United Nations, governments, corporations and more for the purposes of gaining advantages (both economically and militarily)	I, M, E	Rudner	Journal	2013	454
Invested in the capabilities to foster computer network operations (CNO) which more broadly includes computer network exploitation (CNE), and computer network attack (CNA) in order to expose vulnerabilities in targeted nations	I, M, E	Weaver	Journal	2017	10
It has robust military capabilities and is pursuing out-of-area operations as a way to demonstrate strength to the world	M	Weaver	Book	2017	NA
Evidence from secondary sources point to China in particular as being adept at using cyber espionage as a way to infiltrate into government and private sector networks throughout the United States	I, M, E	Weaver	Book	2017	NA

How/Why	D.I.M.E.	Author(s)	Source Type	Date	Page
An assessment of China's People's Liberation Army capability also shows the relevancy of this country's acquisition of systems and capabilities to be used for cyber attacks	I, M	Regional Focus	Systems, and Assessment	2014	NA
Economically, China has been engaged in cyber espionage to com-press the research and development timeline to enhance its position in the world while improv-ing its military capabil-ities	I, M, E	Weaver	Book	2017	NA
A U.S unmanned under-water vehicle (UUV) was seized by China unlaw-fully in the South China Sea while a U.S. Navy oceanographic survey ship was recovering it	M	P.R. 448-16	Press Release	2016	NA
China's intelligence appa-ratus is focused predom-inately on internal oper-ations but it is becoming increasingly concerned with regional and global considerations	I	Crosston	Journal	2016	118
China is concerned with using intelligence to ensure survival of its existence	I	Crosston	Journal	2016	119
China has increased its focus on building and modernizing its military	M	Crosston	Journal	2016	119

How/Why	D.I.M.E.	Author(s)	Source Type	Date	Page
China is working to enhance its own border security while exerting greater maritime influences in the region	M	Crosston	Journal	2016	119
Of notable importance, is the rising military tensions on its border between the two Koreas	M	Crosston	Journal	2016	119
Diplomatically, China has pushed to convince the world that its intentions both regionally and globally are benign	D	Crosston	Journal	2016	120
Much of what China has done underscores its desire to emphasize sovereignty and ostensibly coming across as nonchalant through its contemporary philosophy and cultural leanings	D	Crosston	Journal	2016	120
Moreover, it will likely look to sustainability development and internal consumption over dependence on other nations states	E	Crosston	Journal	2016	121
China is greatly concerned about cybersecurity (CND) to protect itself from exploitation by others	I	Crosston	Journal	2016	124
China supported most of the measures requested by the United States in response to North Korea's September 2017 nuclear tests thereby supporting to U.N. Security Council resolution 2375, tightening the pressure on North Korea	D	UN2375	Government Document	2017	NP

How/Why	D.I.M.E.	Author(s)	Source Type	Date	Page
What is somewhat reassuring is the inextricable linkage of the economies of both China and the United States at least for the foreseeable future	E	WEF	Government Document	2018	NP
This comes at a time when China is looking to maintain state influence over merchants in China; this has occurred in the backdrop of setbacks to liberalization and the press/media sectors; seven industries still remain under the control of the state—telecommunication, petroleum, defense, coal mining, electricity, civil aviation, and ocean shipping	E	Li	Book	2001	NA
China is also interested in enhancing its information technology sector as a way to grow market share in the world in this specific industry	E	WTA	Government Document	2017	4

References

CIA China. (2018). *China.* https://www.cia.gov/library/publications/resources/the-world-factbook/geos/ch.html. Accessed on April 19, 2018.

Crosston, Matthew. (2016). Bringing Non-Western Cultures and Conditions into Comparative Intelligence Perspectives: India, Russia, and China. *International Journal of Intelligence and Counterintelligence.* 29(1): 110–131.

GAO 17-369. (2017). *Actions Needed to Address Five Key Mission Challenges.* http://www.gao.gov/products/gao-17-369. Accessed on July 23, 2017.

Goldman, Merle. (2005). *From Comrades to Citizens: The Struggle for Political Rights in China.* Harvard University Press, Massachusetts USA.

Gries, Peter H. (2004). *China's New Nationalism: Pride, Politics, and Diplomacy.* Berkeley and Los Angeles University Press.

Hu, Angang. (2011). *China in 2020: A New Kind of Superpower.* Washington DC: Brookings Institution Press.

IMF. (2017). *International Monetary Fund World Economic Outlook Database, April 2017.* http://www.imf.org/external/pubs/ft/weo/2017/01/weodata/weorept.aspx?pr.x=32&pr.y=19&sy=2015&ey=2016&scsm=1&ssd=1&sort=country. Accessed on July 18, 2017.

Jalalzai, Musa Khan. (2016). *Fixing the EU Intel Crisis: Intelligence Sharing, Law Enforcement, and the Threat of Chemical Biological, and Nuclear Terrorism.* Algora Publishing.

Joint Press Release. (2017). *Secretary of State Rex Tillerson and Secretary of Defense Jim Mattis at Joint Press Availability June 21, 2017.* https://www.state.gov/secretary/remarks/2017/06/272103.htm. Accessed on July 18, 2017.

Li, Xiaofei. (2010). *China's Outward Foreign Investment A Political Perspective.* University Press of America.

Lowenthal, Mark M. (2017). *Intelligence from Secrets to Policy* (7th Edition). Sage Press.

NDS. (2018). *National Defense Strategy.* https://www.defense.gov/Portals/1/Documents/pubs/2018-National-Defense-Strategy-Summary.pdf. Accessed on January 20, 2018.

OSD. (2017). *Annual Report to Congress: Military and Security Developments Involving the People's Republic of China 2017.* https://www.defense.gov/Portals/1/Documents/pubs/2017_China_Military_Power_Report.PDF. Accessed on July 18, 2017.

P.R. 448-16. (2016). *Statement by Pentagon Press Secretary Peter Cook on Incident in South China Sea.* https://www.defense.gov/News/News-Releases/News-Release-View/Article/1032611/statement-by-pentagon-press-secretary-peter-cook-on-incident-in-south-china-sea/source/GovDelivery/. Accessed on July 27, 2017.

Regional Focus. (2015). *Regional Focus Asia Pacific.* http://www.janes.com/article/39339/regional-focus-asia-pacific-es14e2. Accessed on February 18, 2016. June 17, 2014.

Rogers, Michael. (2017). Admiral Michael S. Rogers (USN), Director, National Security Agency, and Commander, U.S. Cyber Command, Delivers Remarks at The New America Foundation Conference on CYBERSECURITY. https://www.nsa.gov/news-features/speeches-testimonies/speeches/022315-new-america-foundation.shtml. Accessed on July 20, 2017.

Rudner, M. (2013). Cyber-threats to Critical National Infrastructure: an Intelligence Challenge. *International Journal of Intelligence and Counterintelligence.* 36(3): 453–481.

UN. (2014). *UN Data a World of Information.* http://data.un.org/Data.aspx?d=POP&f=tableCode%3a1. Accessed on July 18, 2017.

UN 2375. (2017). *Resolution 2375 North Korea.* http://www.un.org/en/ga/search/view_doc.asp?symbol=S/RES/2375(2017). Accessed on September 26, 2017.

Weaver, John M. (2017). Cyber Threats to the National Security of the United States: A Qualitative Assessment (Chapter). In *Focus on Terrorism (Volume 15).* Nova Science Publishers, New York [(Joshua Morgan (editor)].

WEF. (2018). The Global Risks Report 2018 (13th Edition). *World Economic Forum.* http://www3.weforum.org/docs/WEF_GRR18_Report.pdf. Accessed on January 19, 2018.

White House Press Release 1. (2017). *Readout of President Donald J. Trump's Meeting with President Xi Jinping of China.* https://www.whitehouse.gov/the-press-office/2017/07/08/reado ut-president-donald-j-trumps-meeting-president-xi-jinping-china. Accessed on July 18, 2107.

WTA. (2017). *Worldwide Threat Assessment.* https://www.dni.gov/files/documents/Newsroom/ Testimonies/SSCI%20Unclassified%20SFR%20-%20Final.pdf. Accessed on January 20, 2018.

· 6 ·

FRANCE

History and Background of France

France is a major leader in the European Union (EU) and will likely fill part of the vacuum once the United Kingdom departs from the EU. This country is also one of four countries considered both powerful and influential within the European sphere of influence (Jalalzai, 2016, p. 18). It is also one of the most modern countries in the world exerts significant influence among European nations. France also is a major global powerhouse as a permanent member of the United Nations Security Council, the North Atlantic Treaty Organization, a member of both the G-7 and the G-20, and the EU (CIA, 2018). France rejoined NATO's integrated military command structure back in 2009, reversing President De Gaulle's 1966 decision to withdraw French forces from the alliance (CIA, 2018). Since the late 1950s, it has constructed a hybrid presidential-parliamentary system of governance resistant to the instabilities experienced in previous, administrations that were purely parliamentary in nature (CIA, 2018). France's reconciliation and cooperation with Germany in recent decades have proved to be critical to the integration of Europe economically (Sa'adah, 2003). This has included the introduction of the euro as its currency dating back to January 1999. Five French overseas entities—French Guiana, Guadeloupe, Martinique, Mayotte, and Reunion—became French regions and were made part of France proper in recent decades (McMillan, 2000).

France's government is a semi-presidential republic (McMillan, 2000). The country is broken up into administrative divisions (CIA, 2018). These include 18 regions: (1) Auvergne-Rhone-Alpes, (2) Bourgogne-Franche-Comte (Burgundy-Free County), (3) Bretagne (Brittany), (4) Centre-Val de Loire (Center-Loire Valley), (5) Corse (Corsica), (6) Grand Est (Grand East), (7) Guadeloupe, (8) Guyane (French Guiana), (9) Hauts-de-France (Upper France), (10) Ile-de-France, (11) Martinique, (12) Mayotte, (13) Normandie (Normandy), (14) Nouvelle-Aquitaine (New Aquitaine), (15) Occitanie (Occitania), (16) Pays de la Loire (Lands of the Loire), (17(Provence-Alpes-Cote d'Azur, and (18) Reunion (CIA, 2018). Likewise, the country is further divided into 13 metropolitan regions (and these include the "collectivity" of Corsica or Corse) and five overseas regions (French Guiana, Guadeloupe, Martinique, Mayotte, and Reunion); it is also subdivided into five overseas departments (which are the same as the overseas regions) and 96 metropolitan departments (CIA, 2018).

The country's executive branch consists of the chief of state; at present this is President Emmanuel Macron (CIA, 2018). The head of government is the prime minister, and Minister Edouard Philippe occupies this position (CIA, 2018). The French cabinet is the Council of Ministers and they are subsequently appointed by the president at the suggestion of the Prime Minister (Drake, 2011). The president is directly elected by absolute majority popular vote through two rounds (if needed) for a five year term; the incumbent is eligible for a second term (CIA, 2018).

France has a legislative branch called the bicameral Parliament or Parlement and it consists of the Senate or Senat; it is comprised of 348 seats—328 for metropolitan France and overseas departments and regions of Guadeloupe, Martinque, French Guiana, Reunion, and Mayotte, two for New Caledonia, two for French Polynesia, one for Saint-Pierre and Miquelon, one for Saint-Barthelemy, one for Saint-Martin, one for Wallis and Futuna, and finally, 12 for French nationals residing abroad (CIA, 2018). These members are indirectly elected by departmental electoral colleges requiring an absolute majority vote in two rounds (if needed) for departments with one to three members and proportional representation vote in departments with four or more members; they serve six year terms with one-half of the membership renewed every three years (CIA, 2018). The National Assembly or

Assemblee Nationale has 577 seats of which 556 are for metropolitan France, 10 for departments overseas, and 11 for citizens residing abroad (CIA, 2018); these members are directly elected by absolute majority vote in two rounds (again if needed) to serve five year terms (Drake, 2011).

The French judicial branch's highest court(s) is known as the Court of Cassation or Court de Cassation; it is comprised of the court president, six divisional presiding judges, 120 trial judges, and 70 deputy judges (CIA, 2018). They are organized into six divisions—three of which are civil, one deals with commercial matters, one focuses on labor issues, and one on criminal proceedings; the Constitutional Council has nine members (CIA, 2018). The judge selection and term of office is as follows: the Court of Cassation judges are appointed by the president of the republic by nominations from the High Council of the Judiciary, presided over by the Court of Cassation and 15 appointed members (these judges are appointed for life); Constitutional Council members include three that are appointed by the president of the republic and three by the Senate and National Assembly presidents; members serve 9-year, non-renewable terms with one-third of the membership renewed every three years (CIA, 2018).

France has an economy that is diversified across all sectors. Its government has partially or fully privatized major companies that include the likes of Air France, France Telecom, Renault, and Thales (CIA, 2018). The government of France, however, maintains a position as a strong and influential actor in some sectors, particularly with the power, public transport, and defense sectors (CIA, 2018). France is the most visited country in the world and saw over 83 million foreign tourists in 2016 alone (CIA, 2018). France's leaders in contemporary times, remain committed to capitalism in which they maintain social equity by means of tax policies, laws, and social spending to mitigate economic inequality (Drake, 2011).

France's real gross domestic product (GDP) grew by 1.6% in 2017; this is an upward increase from 1.2% the year before (CIA, 2018). That stated, France's unemployment rate (including its overseas territories) increased from 7.8% in 2008 to 10.2% in 2015, before declining to 9.5% in 2017 (CIA, 2018). Youth unemployment in metropolitan France has also seen a decrease from 24.6% in the fourth quarter of 2014 to 24% in the last quarter of 2016 (CIA, 2018).

France's public finances historically have been strained by significant spending and low growth. Regardless of its initiatives to restore public finances, France's budget deficit rose from 3.3% of GDP in 2008 to 7.5% of

GDP in 2009 (CIA, 2018). In 2017, the budget deficit saw improvements to 2.9% of GDP, bringing it in compliance with the EU mandated 3% deficit target (CIA, 2018). Likewise, France's public debt rose from 89.5% of GDP in 2012 to 96.9% in 2017 (CIA, 2018).

Since assuming office in May 2017, President Emmanuel Macron implemented a series of economic reforms to improve competitiveness and further economic growth (CIA, 2018). President Macron had campaigned on reforming France's labor code and in late 2017 implemented a range of reforms to increase flexibility of its labor market by facilitating a process to make it easier for firms to hire and fire and simplifying negotiations between employees and their employers (CIA, 2018). What's more is that Macron proposed 2018 budget cuts to public spending, taxes, and social security contributions all with the hope of spurring private investment and increase purchasing power (CIA, 2018).

France has a formidable military. Its branches consist of the Army (Armee de Terre) the Marines, Foreign Legion, Army Light Aviation, Navy (Marine Nationale), and Air Force (Armee de l'Air (AdlA) which also includes Air Defense (Drake, 2011).

There are some transnational threats confronting France. Most notably, these include Madagascar and claims of the French territories of Bassas da India, Europa Island, Glorioso Islands, and Juan de Nova Island (CIA, 2018). Moreover, Comoros claims Mayotte; Mauritius has claimed Tromelin Island; territorial dispute also exist between Suriname and the French overseas department of French Guiana; France has also asserted a territorial claim in Antarctica (Adelie Land); France and Vanuatu have both claimed Matthew and Hunter Islands, east of New Caledonia (CIA, 2018).

French Intelligence

Since 2008, France has structured its intelligence community similar to that of the United States. More pointedly, it also has a national intelligence coordinator otherwise referred to as the coordonnateur national du renseignement (CNR) (Lowenthal, 2017). French intelligence is considered both professional and strong, is quite adept at collection, and shares relevant information with those that it considers allies (Jalalzai, 2016, p. 18).

The primary external intelligence arm of France is its Direction Générale de la Sécurité Extérieure or DGSE (Lowenthal, 2017, p. 504). Moreover, the organization consists of four sub directorates. The first of these is strategically oriented and focuses on generating intelligence requirements with input from policy makers (most notably for the Foreign Ministry), and the conduct of intelligence studies (Lowenthal, 2017, p. 505).

The second looks at actual intelligence predominately the collection of information from human intelligence (HUMINT) sources (Lowenthal, 2017). The focus is on not just the exploitation and production of actual intelligence but the subsequent distribution of finished products (Lowenthal, 2017).

Technical collection is the third focal point of the DGSE. It looks to collect signals intelligence (SIGINT), often from ground sites and sensors (Lowenthal, 2017).

Finally, the DGSE executes operations. More specifically, it looks to support clandestine missions the world over.

France's internal intelligence organization is called the Direction Générale de la Sécurité Intérieure (DGSI) and it replaced a precursor organization in 2014 (Lowenthal, 2017). Unlike the DGSE which reports to the Minister of Defense, the DGSI answers to the Minister of the Interior (Lowenthal, 2017). It is primarily responsible for the conduct of such operations as counterintelligence, combating violent extremism and terror, protecting France's industrial base (science, technology, and economic) and also maintains "S files" for files regarding the safety of the state and accordingly has dossiers on people who are possible threats to its country (Lowenthal, 2017).

The country has a military intelligence component as well. The DRM (Direction du Renseignement Militarie or Directorate of Military Intelligence) focuses on threats emanating from other countries' armed forces and threats to their own military structure and includes imagery support to the force (Lowenthal, 2017).

The Direction du renseignement et de la sécurité de la Défense focuses on both counterintelligence and the political reliability of its armed forces by surveillance of its own military (Lowenthal, 2017).

Analysis of France

The United Nations database shows that France ranks 21st overall in the world in terms of population and coming in fourth in relative size to the other four nations in this study by population and is estimated at 67 million people (UN, 2014). France's economic strength as measured by the GDP ranks sixth in the world valued at $2.4 trillion and ranks fourth relative to the other permanent Security Council members (IMF, 2017). France, as a nation, considers national interests more broadly than its other European counterpart, the United Kingdom (Clark, 2017, p. 28).

The rest of this section is dedicated to the application of the YIRTM-M and how it applies to France. Supporting data for this section is found in Annex 6.1. Here one will find the exact breakdown by instruments for the data supporting the analysis section. Likewise, the variation of sources tied back to the Federal Secondary Data Case Study Triangulation Model will also show the balance in sources contributing to the analysis of each instrument of national power.

Diplomatically, France has rolled out the red carpet to endear itself to the United States in July 2017. More pointedly, President Trump was President Marcron's guest of honor during its Bastille Day ceremonies on July 14th (White House Press Release 2, 2017). Macron also used the visit as an opportunity to address issues of joint security, cooperation in cyber defense, and countering terror propaganda (White House Press Release 3, 2017). Likewise, Marcon's country supported President Trump's call for greater sanctions regarding nuclear and ballistic missile tests by North Korea (UN2375, 2017).

France, though, has loosened the application of intelligence resources on its citizenry in recent years. The country's political leadership has allowed for this due to the rising threat of terrorists operating within the country's borders (Hammond, 2015). Among other issues, France has extended the breadth from which it can conduct intelligence missions and by extension the ability to implement mass surveillance of electronic communications (Hammond, 2015). What is challenging though is that France hasn't introduced significant intelligence reform that would lead to the prevention of terror at home (Jalalzai, 2016, p. 13).

The country has also made use of relationships fomented with nations where it once had colonies and has been quite adept at using this in contemporary times (Honig & Zimskind, 2017, p. 432). Conversely, it has been less receptive to accepting intelligence from other nations; the DGSE, for example, failed to seriously consider information received from Arab countries that led up to the November 2015 Paris attacks (Honig & Zimskind, 2017, p. 440).

Prior to the 2017 elections in France, the Office of the Director of National Intelligence (ODNI) and by extension the members of the U.S. intelligence community (IC) assessed that following the U.S. election, Russia would try to influence other democratic elections of allies using cyber (ODNI, 2017, p. iii).

Russia did just this in France. France's electoral system calls for the president to be elected to a five year term directly by the citizens of the country (Election Code, 2017). Though the country uses a paper ballot system, social media and the subsequent promotion of (or slander to) candidates are vulnerable to hacking. In testimony before the Senate Intelligence Community, in direct response to Senator Richard Burr's question on France's preemptive actions during its May 2017 election, Bill Priestap, the Assistant Director for the Federal Bureau of Investigation's (FBI) Counterintelligence Division, referenced that the French did take action but wouldn't elaborate (CSPAN, 2017). More specifically, in a report released by tech security firm Trend Micro showed that Emanuel Macron's campaign successfully took preemptive steps to ward off hacking attempts by a group called Pawn Storm linked to Russia bent on affecting the French elections (Trend Micro, 2017).

With regards to information, France sees utility in sharing information especially as it relates to transnational terrorism. This has been evident in it finalizing information sharing relationships bilaterally with the United States and multilaterally through improved information sharing with the European Union (EU) (DOS, 2017).

Militarily, France has leveraged its armed forces and by extension the relationship of other allies more so in recent years. Hubert Védrine, a former French Minister of Foreign Affairs noted in recent years that France was happy to be back in the NATO military structure and stated that his country had no intention of leaving it again; this is particularly relevant in times of fiscal challenge (Lasconjarias, 2014). France has seen the utility in leveraging capabilities of other countries and the benefits in alliance strengths when confronting major threats abroad.

Yet France has experienced pressure exerted by terrorism. Moreover, it appears that though France has tremendous military capabilities, it remains vulnerable to acts of terror pursuing softer targets. These include the likes of the attacks on Charlie Hebdo in January of 2015, and the major act of terror in Paris France in November 2015 (Jalalzai, 2016, p. 13). In July of 2016, a Tunisian resident using a 19-ton cargo truck killed 86 and injured hundreds more on Bastille Day at a seaside resort (DOS, 2017). This has called into question the utility of the security measures put in place by France (Jalalzai, 2016, p. 18).

France has taken its fight against terror organizations globally and has been a pinnacle actor on the African continent. It has been involved in Operation Barkhaned, a counterterrorism operation in Shahel region working with the U.N. Multinational Integrated Mission in Mali (DOS, 2017). It has also been an instrumental pillar in working with the U.N. to help develop and train counterterrorism forces in Niger (DOS, 2017). It has and continues to support counterterrorism efforts in Libya (DOS, 2017).

France's counterterrorism efforts transcend Africa and include operations in the Middle East. It has been one of the primary contributors to air operations to counter the Islamic State's efforts in both Iraq and Syria (DOS, 2017).

This nation, like most others in the world, has finally emerged from the economic downturn of 2008 (WEF, 2018, p. 6). France, along with the economies of Germany, Italy and the United Kingdom, account for 70% of the total gross domestic product and defense spending of Europe (GAO-02-174, 2001). Economically, France has unique powers. In terms of business and foreign investment, it can impose measures to protect its national security. More specifically, it can do so through the imposition of conditions or the ordering of divestment for activities that it deems as failing within a strategic structure (Clark, 2017, p. 72). Economically, and by extension militarily, foreign investment in this nation's defense sector goes through careful scrutiny (Clark, 2017, p. 70).

France is a key member of the Financial Action Task Force (FATF) and has a dedicated financial intelligence unit called Tracfin (DOS, 2017). It is actively involved in thwarting terror financing and in anti-money laundering activities. The country's efforts include measures designed to limit anonymous cash transactions, to improve suspicious transaction tracking, and asset freezing (DOS, 2017).

Implications for Intelligence Professionals

France has been a valued ally of the United States for over two centuries. In recent times, diplomatic relations between the two nations is at the strongest level than one has seen in recent years. Intelligence professionals should see this as an opportunity to support alliances as the United States, France and others look to form coalitions against like-minded threats like those found in Syria, to counter Islamic extremists and to strengthen the position of NATO in Eastern Europe. The global intelligence community should also realize that France will most likely support United Nations' resolutions that will help mitigate existential threats like those posed by North Korea.

This country is concerned with the proliferation of attacks at home and accordingly, has increasingly turned to its intelligence services to collect information at home and abroad. The DGSI will continue to monitor activity on France's Homefront. Under the CNR, the DGSE will focus efforts abroad to collect intelligence on those beyond its borders looking to harm it. It is also interested in protecting the integrity of its government and by extension its elections. Intelligence professionals in the United States should continue to work with the French especially with regards to the threat posed by Islamic extremists and share information bilaterally. Based on this high point of relations between the United States and France, U.S. intelligence should request assistance regarding terror organizations operating in Africa as it looks to increase its counter terrorism efforts on this continent. France will be interested in partnering with other nations to share information on election tampering to protect it and other democracies throughout the world. Likewise, other intelligence services allied to France can turn to this nation in order to request intelligence analysis derived from former French colonies (and human sources) the world over. Moreover, France views terror as a global threat and can be counted on to support U.N. initiatives aimed at countering terrorism.

France will continue to leverage its military especially with the intention of pursuing terror threats abroad to degrade and destroy them to minimize the likelihood that these nefarious groups find their way into the country. Intelligence professionals in the United States and globally will continue to see that France values NATO as a potent organization in order to benefit from shared capabilities and costs associated with taking out targets (especially those associated with transnational terror organizations like the Islamic State). It will also support UNSC initiatives to counter threats pertaining to terrorism, and weapons of mass destruction like the chemical attacks used in Syria, and North Korea's pursuit of ballistic missile technology and its nuclear weapons' program.

It will seek to either maintain or improve its economic interests by assuming a more assertive leadership role in the European Union (with the departure of the United Kingdom) and will also look to shore up bilateral arrangements with other nations to improve its economy. France will likely use its colonial ties and its intelligence services to conduct threat analysis especially in the context of transnational terrorism to pursue trade agreements that will benefit France while avoiding arrangements with countries that are seen as unstable or susceptible to terrorism.

Annex 6.1 France

How/Why	D.I.M.E.	Author(s)	Source Type	Date	Page
France makes diplomatic overtures to endear itself to the U.S.	D	White House Press Release 2	Press Release	2017	NA
Joint security, cooperation in cyber defense, and countering terror propaganda	D, I, M, E	White House Press Release 3	Press Release	2017	NA
Russia would try to influence other democratic elections of allies using cyber	D, I	ODNI	Government Document	2017	iii
References to action by the French to preemptively prevent Russian hacking during May 2017 election	I	CSPAN	Testimony	2017	NA
Electoral System makes use of paper ballot; social media is still vulnerable	I	Electoral Code	System	2017	NA
In a report released by tech security firm Trend Micro showed that Emanuel Macron's campaign successfully took preemptive steps to ward off hacking attempts by a group called Pawn Storm linked to Russia bent on affecting the French elections	I	Trend Micro	Report	2017	NA
Hubert Védrine, a former French Minister of Foreign Affairs noted in recent years that France was happy to be back in the NATO military structure and stated that his country had no intent of leaving it again; this is particularly relevant in times of fiscal challenge	D, M, E	Lasconjarias	Journal	2014	NA

How/Why	D.I.M.E.	Author(s)	Source Type	Date	Page
The country's political leadership has allowed for this due to the rising threat of terrorists operating within its country's borders. Among other issues, France has extended the breadth from which it can conduct intelligence missions and by extension the ability to implement mass surveillance of electronic communications	D, I	Hammond	Document	2015	NA
The country has also made use of relationships fomented with nations where it had colonies and has been quite adept at using this in contemporary times	I	Honig & Zimskind	Journal	2017	432
France has been less receptive to accepting intelligence from other nations; the DGSE, for example, failed to seriously consider information received from Arab countries that led up to the November 2015 Paris attacks	I	Honig & Zimskind	Journal	2017	440
Marcon's country supported President Trump's call for greater sanctions regarding recent nuclear and ballistic missile tests by North Korea	D	UN2375	Government Document	2017	NP

How/Why	D.I.M.E.	Author(s)	Source Type	Date	Page
Imposition of conditions or the ordering of divestment for activities that it deems as failing within a strategic structure	E	Clark	Government Document	2017	72
Economically, and by extension, militarily foreign investment in this nation's defense sector goes through careful scrutiny	M, E	Clark	Government Document	2017	70
France, along with the economies of Germany, Italy and the United Kingdom account for 70% of the total gross domestic product and defense spending of Europe	M, E	GAO-02-174	Government Document	2001	20
Cargo truck killed 86 and injured hundreds more on Bastille Day at a seaside resort	M	DOS	Government Document	2017	2
France has been involved in counterterrorism efforts in African and more specifically in Mali, Niger, and Libya	M	DOS	Government Document	2017	4, 46, 117
This country has been instrumental in air support operations against the Islamic State throughout the Middle East and most notably in both Iraq and Syria	M	DOS	Government Document	2017	116
France has improved information sharing relationships U.S. and the E.U.	I	DOS	Government Document	2017	118

How/Why	D.I.M.E.	Author(s)	Source Type	Date	Page
France is a key member of the Financial Action Task Force (FATF) and has a dedicated financial intelligence unit called Tracfin	E	DOS	Government Document	2017	119
Measures to counter terrorism include limiting anonymous cash transactions, to improving suspicious transaction tracking, and asset freezing	E	DOS	Government Document	2017	119

References

CIA. (2018). *France.* https://www.cia.gov/library/publications/resources/the-world-factbook/geos/fr.html. Accessed on April 19, 2018.

Clark, Greg. (2017). *National Security and Infrastructure Investment Review.* Department for Business, Energy & Industrial Strategy, United Kingdom. https://www.gov.uk/government/consultations/national-security-and-infrastructure-investment-review. Accessed on October 17, 2017.

CSPAN. (2017). *Russian Interference in U.S. Elections.* https://www.c-span.org/video/?430128-1/senate-intel-panel-told-21-states-targeted-russia-2016-election. Accessed on July 23, 2017.

DOS2. (2017). *Country Reports on Terrorism 2016.* Department of State. https://www.state.gov/j/ct/rls/crt/2016/index.htm. Accessed on October 17, 2017.

Drake, H. (2011). *Contemporary France.* London.

Election Code. (2017). Legifrance. https://www.legifrance.gouv.fr/affichCodeArticle.do?idArticle=LEGIARTI000006353155&cidTexte=LEGITEXT000006070239. Accessed on July 23, 2107.

GAO-02-174. (2001). *European Security U.S. and European Contributions to Foster Stability and Security in Europe.* https://www.gpo.gov/fdsys/pkg/GAOREPORTS-GAO-02-174/pdf/GAOREPORTS-GAO-02-174.pdf. Accessed on October 17, 2017.

Hammond, Brian. (2015). French National Assembly Clears Bill to Expand Government. *Cybersecurity Policy Report.* Aspen Publishers, Inc.

Honig, Or and Sarah Zimskind. (2017). The Spy Machine and the Ballot Box: Examining Democracy's Intelligence Advantage. *International Journal of Intelligence and Counterintelligence.* 3(3): 431–463.

IMF. (2017). *International Monetary Fund World Economic Outlook Database, April 2017*. http://www.imf.org/external/pubs/ft/weo/2017/01/weodata/weorept.aspx?pr.x=32&pr.y=19&sy=2015&ey=2016&scsm=1&ssd=1&sort=country. Accessed on July 18, 2017.

Jalalzai, Musa Khan. (2016). *Fixing the EU Intel Crisis: Intelligence Sharing, Law Enforcement, and the Threat of Chemical Biological, and Nuclear Terrorism*. Algora Publishing.

Lasconjarias, Guillaume. (2014). 'Rentrée dans le rang?' France, NATO and the EU, from the Védrine report to the 2013 French White Paper on national security and defence. *Journal of Transatlantic Studies*. 12(4): 418–431.

Lowenthal, Mark M. (2017). *Intelligence from Secrets to Policy* (7th Edition). Sage Press.

McMillan, J. (2000). *Modern France*. Oxford Press.

ODNI. (2017). *Background to "Assessing Russian Activities and Intentions in Recent US Elections": The Analytic Process and Cyber Incident Attribution*. https://www.documentcloud.org/documents/3254239-Russia-Hacking-report.html. Accessed on July 20, 2017.

Sa'adah A. (2003). *Contemporary France: A Democratic Education*. Oxford Press.

Trend Micro. (2017). From Espionage to Cyber Propaganda: Pawn Storm's Activities over the Past Two Years. https://www.trendmicro.com/vinfo/us/security/news/cyber-attacks/espionage-cyber-propaganda-two-years-of-pawn-storm. Accessed on July 27, 2017.

UN. (2014). *UN Data a World of Information*. http://data.un.org/Data.aspx?d=POP&f=tableCode%3a1. Accessed on July 18, 2017.

UN 2375. (2017). *Resolution 2375 North Korea*. http://www.un.org/en/ga/search/view_doc.asp?symbol=S/RES/2375(2017). Accessed on September 26, 2017.

WEF. (2018). *The Global Risks Report 2018* (13th Edition). World Economic Forum. http://www3.weforum.org/docs/WEF_GRR18_Report.pdf. Accessed on January 19, 2018.

White House Press Release 2. (2017). *President Trump in Paris: Day 2*. https://www.whitehouse.gov/blog/2017/07/14/president-trump-paris-day-2. Accessed on July 18, 2017.

White House Press Release 3. (2017). *Remarks by President Trump and President Macron of France in Joint Press Conference. July 13, 2017*. https://www.whitehouse.gov/the-press-office/2017/07/13/remarks-president-trump-and-president-macron-france-joint-press. Accessed on July 18, 2017.

· 7 ·

RUSSIA

History and Background of Russia

Russia experienced a series of devastating defeats of its military in World War I; this led to significant rioting in the major cities of the Russian Empire. It resulted in the overthrow of the imperial household in 1917 (CIA, 2018). Vladimir Lenin and his communists seized power soon after and formed the USSR and subsequently the brutal rule under his successor, Iosif Stalin from 1928 to 1953, and fomented communist rule and the Russian dominance of the Soviet Union at a cost of tens of millions of lives (CIA, 2018). Following Germany's defeat in World War II as part of an alliance with the United States, it expanded its territory into Eastern Europe as a way to create a buffer between western aligned countries and Russia's own western border. Following World War II, the USSR became a global power and was the principle antagonist to the United States until the end of the Cold War in 1991. The Soviet society and economy atrophied in the decades following Stalin's rule, until General Secretary Mikhail Gorbachev, who ruled from 1985 until 1991, introduced the concepts of glasnost (openness) and perestroika (restructuring) in an attempt to modernize communism; these initiatives were seen as the nexus that inadvertently released forces splintering the USSR into Russia and 14 other independent republics (CIA, 2018).

Following the economic and political turmoil during President Boris Yeltsin's time in office, ruling from 1991 until 1999, Russia made its shift toward a centralized authoritarian state under the leadership of President Vladimir Putin (Lourie, 2017). Subsequently, Putin's regime has sought to legitimize its rule through populist appeals, managed elections, a foreign policy focused on enhancing the country's geopolitical influence, and economic growth that is based in large part on commodities (Goldman, 2008).

Russia's executive branch consists of the president (Jack, 2004). Since May of 2012, Vladimir Vladimirovich Putin has been in office. This branch also consists of the head of government: Premier Dmitriy Mendevev, the First Deputy Premier, Igor Shuvalov, and eight Deputy Premiers—Arkadiy Dvorkovich, Olga Golodets, Aleksandr Khloponin, Dmitriy Kozak, Vitaliy Mutko, Dmitriy Rogozin, Sergey Prikhodko and Yuriy Trutnev (CIA, 2018). Moreover, the cabinet, otherwise referred to as the "Government," is made up by the premier, his deputies, and ministers, all of whom are appointed by the president; the premier is also confirmed by the Duma (Jack, 2004).

The president is directly elected by absolute majority popular vote in two rounds if needed for a term of six years and remains eligible to serve for a second term (Jack, 2004). Administratively, the Presidential Administration provides policy and staff to the president, it drafts presidential decrees, and also coordinates policy among various government agencies; a Security Council also answers directly to the president (CIA, 2018).

Russia's legislative branch is a bicameral Federal Assembly or otherwise known as the Federalnoye Sobraniye; it consists of the Federation Council or Sovet Federatsii (with 170 seats; two members in each of the 83 federal administrative units). The federal council overseeing the oblasts, krays, republics, autonomous okrugs and oblasts, and the federal cities of Moscow and Saint Petersburg are appointed by the top executive and legislative officials (CIA, 2018). Its members serve four year terms, while the State Duma or Gosudarstvennaya Duma (which has 450 seats) where half of the members are elected directly by simple majority vote and the other half are directly elected by proportional representation vote; members serve five year terms (CIA, 2018).

The country's judicial branch consists of a Supreme Court of the Russian Federation (made up by 170 members that are organized into the (1) Judicial Panel for Civil Affairs, (2) the Judicial Panel for Criminal Affairs, and the

(3) Military Panel (CIA, 2018). Judges are nominated by the president and appointed by the Federal Council; members of all three are appointed for life.

Russia's economy is nothing like it was at the end of the Cold War. It has seen many changes since the collapse of the Soviet Union and has subsequently moved from a centrally planned economy towards one that is more market-based (Gustafson, 2012). Both reforms and economic growth have become more stagnant in recent years (CIA, 2018). That stated, it is an economy with one of the highest concentration of wealth in officials' hands (Goldman, 2008). Though the economic reformation that took place in the 1990s privatized most industry, there were notable exceptions; these were found in the sectors of energy, banking, transportation, and defense-related industries (Jack, 2004). The protection of property rights in this country is still quite weak, and the state continues to inject its influence into the free operation of the private sector (CIA, 2018).

Russia is one of the world's leading producers of oil and natural gas (ranked second behind Saudi Arabia), and is also one of the top exporters of metals such as aluminum and steel (CIA, 2018). This country is also heavily dependent on the commodity price swings and accordingly, this makes it vulnerable to booms and busts associated with the cyclic nature of the market (Goldman, 2008). Economically, Russia averaged 7% annual growth during the 1998–2008 period as oil prices rose rapidly, but this has diminished in more recent years as a result of the exhaustion of Russia's commodity-based growth model (CIA, 2018).

The amalgamation of international sanctions, falling oil prices, and structural limitations cajoled Russia into a deep recession in 2015, with GDP spiraling downward by close by 2.8%. The downturn continued through calendar year 2016, but has reversed slightly in 2017 as world demand for Russian exports increased (CIA, 2018).

Russia has invested roughly 5.8% of its GDP in defense spending. Its armed forces consists of ground troops (Sukhoputnyye Voyskia, SV), a navy (Voyenno-Morskoy Flot, VMF), and the Aerospace Forces (Vozdushno-Kosmicheskiye Sily, VKS) (CIA, 2018). Conversely, its airborne troops (Vozdushno-Desantnyye Voyska, VDV) and Missile Troops of Strategic Purpose (Raketnyye Voyska Strategicheskogo Naznacheniya, RVSN) referred to commonly as Strategic Rocket Forces, are independent "combat arms," not subordinate to any of the three branches (CIA, 2018).

There are several transnational issues confronting Russia; it remains concerned about the smuggling of poppy derivatives from Afghanistan through

Central Asian countries (CIA, 2018). Likewise Russia and China have demarcated the once disputed islands' confluence at the Amur and Ussuri and in the Argun River in accordance with a ratified 2004 agreement, ending the centuries-long border disputes between these two countries (CIA, 2018).

Maritime disputes continue between Russia and Japan. Specifically the sovereignty dispute over the islands of Etorofu, Kunashiri, Habomai group, and Shikotan, referred as the "Northern Territories" by Japan and in Russia as the "Southern Kurils," occupied by the Soviet Union dating back to 1945, now administered by Russia, and still claimed by Japan, remains the primary friction point to signing a peace treaty formally ending World War II hostilities (CIA, 2018).

Russia's military support and subsequent recognition in 2008 of South Ossetia and Abkhazia independence has created a point of consternation with the country of Georgia (CIA, 2018). Other territorial disputes exist between Russia and the countries of Iran, Finland, and Estonia (CIA, 2018). Finally, Russia still remains involved in the conflict in eastern Ukraine while also occupying Ukraine's territory of Crimea despite calls for Russia to withdraw from leaders of the international community.

Russian Intelligence

Russia is a near-peer rival to the United States with regards to intelligence capabilities (Lowenthal, 2017, p. 516). Historically, it has had a quite competent intelligence service (Albats, 1994). Like the U.S., it has a varied mix of capabilities ranging from human intelligence (HUMINT), counterintelligence, signals intelligence (SIGINT), and imagery intelligence (IMINT) with the capacity to conduct foreign based operations and support to domestic security (Lowenthal, 2017).

Following the Cold War, the Sluzhba Vneshnei Razvedki (SVR) emerged from the former KGB as the organization that provides foreign (or external) intelligence support to Russia (Gessen, 1997). More pointedly, it has the responsibility to conduct HUMINT, industrial espionage, and intelligence liaison functions (Lowenthal, 2017). In recent years Putin has asserted that the SVR will become increasingly relevant to supporting Russia's security because of threats that it perceives coming from western nations (Lowenthal, 2017).

The Federalnaya Sluzhba Bezopasnosti (FSB), has primacy over counterintelligence, internal security, and civil counterespionage (Gessen, 2004).

In the last two decades, the FSB's responsibilities have increased. It is now also responsible for exerting control over its border guards, cryptography, and SIGINT (Lowenthal, 2017).

Russia's Glavnoje Razvedyvatel'noje Upravlenije (GRU) is predominately focused on military intelligence for Russia's armed forces. Under Putin, its power has waned and has seen cuts to its budget and allegations have linked this to the GRU's lack of control of Spetsnaz (the Russian special operations forces) and some opposition by senior leaders in the organization to Putin (Lowenthal, 2017).

Russia has put a high value on its intelligence personnel. Estimates show that 40% of the totality of Russia's bureaucracy and 60% of Putin's administration either have links to intelligence or security backgrounds (Lowenthal, 2017).

Regardless of economic challenges experienced by the country, Russia still has an extensive foreign based intelligence presence (Lourie, 2017). Several countries have reported on Russia's increased activity and these include Canada, Denmark, Germany, Sweden, the Czech Republic, and the United Kingdom (Lowenthal, 2017).

Analysis of Russia

Russia's population shows a ranking in the top 10 worldwide (actual ranking 9th overall) and comes in the middle of the five permanent Security Council members of the United Nations when looking at population numbers (UN, 2014). It is considered to be a growing power (Jalalzai, 2016, p. 18). Russia's GDP value places it at 12th in the world with a value of 1.2 trillion according to the IMF; it comes in last in relation to the other permanent Security Council members (IMF, 2017). The latest edition of the National Defense Strategy of the United States underscores border violations carried out by Russia and using its veto power in the United Nations Security Council to counter diplomatic, military, and economic decisions of its neighbors (NDS, 2018, p. 1).

The rest of this section is dedicated to the application of the YIRTM-M and how it applies to Russia. Supporting data for this section is found in Annex 7.1. Here one will find the exact breakdown by instrument for the data supporting the analysis section. Likewise, the variation of sources tied back to the Federal Secondary Data Case Study Triangulation Model will also show the balance in sources contributing to the analysis of each instrument of national power.

Diplomatically (and militarily), Russia has looked to exert greater influence in the Central Asian States and in the Middle East in recent years (Crosston, 2016, p. 123). This has been evident in its forays into Syria, and through the sales of military equipment to Iran and other outreach activities. Though Russia is in disagreement with the United States and didn't support the full measures requested by the U.S. regarding recent nuclear tests by North Korea, it did affirm support to U.N. Security Council resolution 2375, tightening the pressure on North Korea (UN2375, 2017).

Russia has invested heavily on protecting itself from those looking to gain information (and by extension, intelligence) on its intentions. This underscores the effectiveness of the SVR, FSB, and GRU. It has invested heavily in capabilities to thwart others through its Counterintelligence Service and its Directorate of Military Counterintelligence (Crosston, 2016, p. 123).

Russia has been investing in asymmetric TTPs and has proven quite adept at using cyber as a successful tool making good use of information (and its technology) to its advantage. An unclassified assessment by the intelligence community underscores this with regards to the most recent U.S. federal election (ODNI, 2017). In the key judgment section of the document made available to the public, the intelligence assessment stated that President Putin ordered a campaign with the aim of undermining liberal democratic order while also working to reduce the faith of the U.S. population on the voting process (ODNI, 2017, p. ii). The Russian government was able to do so by using a blend of covert and overt information with a desire to discredit the democratic candidate, Hillary Clinton (ODNI, 2017, p. ii). Senator Mark Warner during an open intelligence hearing where testimony took place, stated that Russia had successfully spread fake news, hacked political emails and leaked them selectively, flooded social media, and all without firing a shot and at very little monetary cost to Russia, regarding the Russian interference in U.S. elections (CSPAN, 2017). Bill Priestap also stated that the Russian spy agency, the GRU, was directly involved in this effort (CSPAN, 2017).

Russia's cyber and information influences transcend elections and include frequent attacks on U.S. private and public sector organizations in discussion that occurred with the director of the NSA (Rogers, 2017). The intelligence community assesses it as a major cyber player on the world stage (WTA, 2017, p. 1). Like China, it has invested in CNE and CNA capabilities in order to steal away secrets from other countries to gain advantages (Weaver, 2017, p. 10). Likewise, it is greatly concerned about cybersecurity (CND) to protect itself from exploitation by others (Crosston, 2016, p. 124).

While it is engaged in cyber espionage, it is shoring up its computer network defenses; this was stated in a released Russian cyber defense plan in December 2016 (Russia Plan, 2016). It most likely has the desire to advance its position diplomatically. Further discussion with the most recent former head of the NSA revealed that this has resulted in the loss of billions of dollars and even state secrets (Rogers, 2017). Bill Priestap also testified before the Senate Intelligence Committee stating that Russia knows that it can't confront the U.S. directly with its military and is investing in cyber as a way to weaken this nation and its allies (CSPAN, 2017). Looking to a NATO ally, Mr. Hjort Frederiksen, Denmark's Defence Minister stated, "This is part of a continuing war from the Russian side in this field, where we are seeing a very aggressive Russia" in response to Russia's attack on its military networks (MacFarquhar, 2017). Though Russia wasn't able to access classified material, the actions were still troubling. The U.S. intelligence community has assessed that it will continue to use cyber as a way to implement information operations to affect diplomatic initiatives and military operations around the world (WTA, 2017, p. 1). Russia's use of cyber as an espionage tool has helped leverage its asymmetric military capabilities while looking for vulnerabilities in U.S. military systems (Weaver, 2017a).

Russia has been quite adept in the past in recruiting foreign agents. However, in recent years, it hasn't been as successful as was shown when its diplomats tried to recruit recent college students in New York (Honig & Zimskind, 2017, p. 453). Whereas it hasn't been as successful at recruiting individuals from the United States and other permanent members of the Security Council, it has seen utility in using propaganda and information to garner support to its causes (Fitzgerald & Brantly, 2017, p. 230). It has also been quite competent at countering NATO's information campaigns to dispel Russian inaccuracies in Ukraine (Fitzgerald & Brantly, 2017, p. 230). According to the latest National Defense Strategy of the United States, it is doing so to shatter this alliance (NDS, 2018, p. 2).

Likewise, Russia has aspirations to show that it is a global power (Crosston, 2016, p. 123). Militarily, this country has been asserting its aggression on the European continent (GAO 17-369, 2017, p. 2). To hedge against allied aggression, Russia has been bolstering the defenses of its friends. In a statement in mid-December of 2016, Russian Foreign Minister Sergey Lavrov said that the Kremlin is currently poised to boost Serbia's defensive capabilities in light of what his Serbian counterpart alleges is a threat from its neighbor— Croatia (Stojanovic, 2016). In doing so, the U.S. has pressured European allies to contribute more to the North Atlantic Treaty Organization (NATO) but in doing so, might hinder economic growth in the region (GAO 17-369, 2017, p. 2).

Staying on the military instrument, Russia, like China, has extensive military capabilities and is pursuing out-of-area operations as a way to demonstrate its strength globally (Weaver, 2017a). It has been instrumental in fighting terrorists in Syria. It has used its military to reposition itself as a major actor in today's world (WEF, 2018, p. 38). Through this, it has tipped its hand in support of Bashar al-Asad's regime and targeted fighters backed by the United States. Other evidence emanating from secondary sources show that Russia is particularly competent at using cyber espionage as a way to infiltrate into government and private sector networks throughout the United States (Weaver, 2017a).

Russia can generate hard currency through weapons' sales as a way to improve its economic position. It can also leverage petroleum shipments to many of the Eastern European countries to serve as a hedging mechanism countering NATO's influences in the region. Though the latter is subject to commodity fluctuations, Russia's account of the worldwide arms sales equates to over 15% of the total market sales and represents a significant source of revenue. It will generate most of its hard currency from the sale of oil, gas, steal, and aluminum. That stated, market fluctuations with commodities will impact Russia economically. For it to remain potent militarily, its economy must grow.

Implications for Intelligence Professionals

Intelligence professionals should look at Russia's diplomatic pursuits through the eyes of history. This country has experience hardship and foreign military invasions in the past and would like to have buffers to add a layer of security to ensure its safety. To help Russia understand what is occurring, it will turn to the members of the FSB and SVR to better understand what is occurring domestically globally. Accordingly, intelligence professionals in the United States, NATO, and the world will likely see the continuance of relations to the Central Asian States, those formerly aligned with the Soviet Union, and even those that are even members of NATO, like Turkey.

Global intelligence services should see this diplomatic engagement by Russia as a way to create not just buffer zones from those that it perceives as threats but also to sow seeds of distrust within organizations that it sees as existential threats like NATO. When looking at Russia's actions through the lens of the UNSC in the context of intelligence, this country will only support efforts that will support its agenda of creating layers of defense in depth and measures that will not weaken it or conversely, strengthen the United States, France, and the United Kingdom (who it views as threats because of its perception of NATO).

Similar to what the analysis showed with China, Russia too will use it intelligence services to both gain information (both from open sources and through surreptitious means) to figure out how they are planning to weaken or hurt it while also looking for ways to improve their technology to serve as a counterbalance to the United States (and its allies); the intelligence organizations of the United States and others should realize this. Likewise, intelligence professionals should note that Russia will invest in cyber TTPs to hedge against western technology by exploiting weaknesses in western public & private networks, industrial bases, and military capabilities.

In recent years, this nations realizes that the over reliance on cyber is an inherent weakness by more advanced nations especially when adequate CND measures are in place. Like China, Russia sees cyber as an equalizing force and will likely push back against U.N. efforts aimed at limiting cyber espionage activities.

Russia sees its military strength as its singular best bet to be viewed as a significant world player. The GRU will be very instrumental in helping the military and though it has seen a reduction in power in recent years, Putin will most likely appoint those loyal to him to prominent positions within this service. Intelligence professionals should note that it will look to military sales as a way to wield power and influence over the world and as a way to improve its generation of hard currency.

It has also demonstrated adeptness at projecting military power both within its region (Crimea), and out of the European area (Syria) in recent years. Russia could continue to use its military power projection as a way to remind the world that it is a formidable country not to be taken lightly.

Moreover, in recent years, the world has seen Russia moving to a more hybrid military assertiveness tied to the uses of quasi-military contractors to obfuscate its true intentions. Though this has had mixed results, it demonstrates that Russia is looking to learn and improve and intelligence professionals should continue to monitor this.

Economically, and linked to the military, Russia will look to its foreign military sales program as a way to improve its economy. Intelligence professionals should look to see what type of economic relations are being pursued by this country to see where it might be fomenting relations especially if the intended outlets for this equipment could be viewed as potential belligerents. Russia has some of the most advance weapons systems like the S-400 anti aircraft system which could pose a threat to aircraft used by the United States and others against such countries as Iran and Syria. Intelligence professional, likewise should constantly monitor the commodities marked because pricing on such products as oil, natural gas, steal and aluminum will have an impact on Russia's economy as well.

Annex 7.1 Russia

How/Why	D.I.M.E.	Author(s)	Source Type	Date	Page
Undermining liberal democratic order while also working to reduce the faith of the U.S. population on the voting process	D, I	ODNI	Government Document	2017	ii
Russian government was able to do so by using a blend of covert and overt information	D, I	ODNI	Government Document	2017	ii
Russia has been asserting its aggression on the European continent	M, E	GAO 17-369	Government Document	2017	2
Pressure on European allies to contribute more to NATO militarily, but in doing so, might hinder economic growth in the region	I, E	GAO 17-369	Government Document	2017	2
Cyber and information influences transcend election and include frequent attacks on U.S. private and public sector organizations	I, E	Rogers	Speech	2017	NA
Russia had successfully spread fake news, hacking of political emails and leaking them selectively, flooded social media, and all without firing a shot with very little money	D, I	CSPAN	Testimony	2017	NA

How/Why	D.I.M.E.	Author(s)	Source Type	Date	Page
It has invested in CNE and CNA capabilities in order to steal away secrets from other countries to gain advantages	D	Weaver	Journal	2017b	10
Has extensive military capabilities and is pursuing out-of-area operations as a way to demonstrate its strength globally	M	Weaver	Book	2017a	NA
Other evidence emanating from secondary sources show that Russia is particularly competent at using cyber espionage as a way to infiltrate into government and private sector networks throughout the United States	I, M, E	Weaver	Book	2017a	NA
Economically, Russia's use of cyber as an espionage tool has helped leverage its asymmetric military capabilities while looking for vulnerabilities in U.S. military systems	I, M, E	Weaver	Book	2017a	NA
While it is engaged in cyber espionage, it is shoring up its computer network defenses; it released a cyber defense plan in December 2016	I, M	Russia Plan	Plan	2016	NA
Russian Foreign Minister Sergey Lavrov said that the Kremlin is currently poised to boost Serbia's defensive capabilities in light of what his Serbian counterpart alleges is a threat from its neighbor—Croatia	M	Stojanovic	Statement	2016	NA
Russia, in recent years hasn't been as successful as was shown when its diplomats tried to recruit recent college students in New York	D, I	Honig & Zimskind	Journal	2017	453

How/Why	D.I.M.E.	Author(s)	Source Type	Date	Page
Whereas Russia hasn't been as successful at recruiting individuals from the United States and other permanent members of the Security Council, it has seen utility in using propaganda and information to garner support to its causes	I	Fitzgerald & Brantly	Journal	2017	230
It has also been quite competent to countering NATO's information campaigns to dispel Russian inaccuracies in Ukraine	I	Fitzgerald & Brantly	Journal	2017	230
Russia has invested heavily on protecting itself from those looking to gain information (and by extension, intelligence) on its intentions.	I	Crosston	Journal	2016	123
It has invested heavily in capabilities to thwart others through its Counterintelligence Service and its Directorate of Military Counterintelligence	I	Crosston	Journal	2016	123
Diplomatically (and militarily), Russia has looked to exert greater influence in the Central Asian States and in the Middle East in recent years	D, M	Crosston	Journal	2016	123
Russia has aspirations to show that it is a global power	D, M	Crosston	Journal	2016	123
Russia has concerns about cybersecurity (CND) to protect itself from exploitation by others	I	Crosston	Journal	2016	124
Russian supported U.N. Security Council resolution 2375, tightening the pressure on North Korea as a result of a recent nuclear test	D	UN2375	Government Document	2017	NP

References

Albats, Yevgeniya. (1994). *The State Within a State: the KGB and its hold on Russia—Past, Present, and Future*. Christian Science Monitor, Boston Massachusetts.

CIA. (2018). *Russia*. https://www.cia.gov/library/publications/resources/the-world-factbook/geos/rs.html. Accessed on April 20, 2018.

Crosston, Matthew. (2016). Bringing Non-Western Cultures and Conditions into Comparative Intelligence Perspectives: India, Russia, and China. *International Journal of Intelligence and Counterintelligence*. 29(1): 110–131.

CSPAN. (2017). *Russian Interference in U.S. Elections*. https://www.c-span.org/video/?430128-1/senate-intel-panel-told-21-states-targeted-russia-2016-election. Accessed on July 23, 2017.

Fitzgerald, Chad W. and Aaron F. Brantly. (2017). Subverting Reality: The Role of Propaganda in 21st Century Intelligence. *International Journal of Intelligence and Counterintelligence*. 3(2): 215–240.

GAO 17-369. (2017). *Actions Needed to Address Five Key Mission Challenges*. http://www.gao.gov/products/gao-17-369. Accessed on July 23, 2017.

Gessen, Masha. (1997). *Dead Again: The Russian Intelligentsia After Communism*. Verso, United Kingdom.

Goldman, Marshall I. (2008). *Petrostate: Putin, Power, and the New Russia*. Oxford Press.

Gustafson, Thane. (2012). *Wheel of Fortune: The Battle for Oil and Power in Russia*. Belknap Press.

Honig, Or and Sarah Zimskind. (2017). The Spy Machine and the Ballot Box: Examining Democracy's Intelligence Advantage. *International Journal of Intelligence and Counterintelligence*. 3(3): 431–463.

IMF. (2017). *International Monetary Fund World Economic Outlook Database, April 18, 2017*. http://www.imf.org/external/pubs/ft/weo/2017/01/weodata/weorept.aspx?pr.x=32&pr.y=19&sy=2015&ey=2016&scsm=1&ssd=1&sort=country. Accessed on July 18, 2017.

Jack, Andrew. (2004). *Inside Putin's Russia*. Oxford University Press.

Jalalzai, Musa Khan. (2016). *Fixing the EU Intel Crisis: Intelligence Sharing, Law Enforcement, and the Threat of Chemical Biological, and Nuclear Terrorism*. Algora Publishing.

Lourie, Richard. (2017). *Putin: His Downfall and Russia's Coming Crash*. St. Martin's Press.

Lowenthal, Mark M. (2017). *Intelligence from Secrets to Policy* (7th Edition). Sage Press.

MacFarquhar, Neil. (2017). *Denmark Says 'Key Elements' of Russian Government Hacked Defense Ministry*. https://www.nytimes.com/2017/04/24/world/europe/russia-denmark-hacking-cyberattack-defense-ministry.html. Accessed on July 27, 2017.

NDS. (2018). *National Defense Strategy*. https://www.defense.gov/Portals/1/Documents/pubs/2018-National-Defense-Strategy-Summary.pdf. Accessed on January 20, 2018.

ODNI. (2017). *Background to "Assessing Russian Activities and Intentions in Recent US Elections": The Analytic Process and Cyber Incident Attribution*. https://www.documentcloud.org/documents/3254239-Russia-Hacking-report.html. Accessed on July 20, 2017.

Rogers, Michael. (2017). *Admiral Michael S. Rogers (USN), Director, National Security Agency, and Commander, U.S. Cyber Command, Delivers Remarks at The New America Foundation Conference on CYBERSECURITY.* https://www.nsa.gov/news-features/speeches-testimonies/speeches/022315-new-america-foundation.shtml. Accessed on July 20, 2017.

Stojanovic, Dusan. (2016). Russia Ready to Boost Serbian Defense to Counter NATO. *U.S. News and World Report.* https://www.usnews.com/news/world/articles/2016-12-12/russia-ready-to-boost-serbian-defense-to-counter-nato. Accessed on July 27, 2017.

UN. (2014). *UN Data a World of Information.* http://data.un.org/Data.aspx?d=POP&f=tableCode%3a1. Accessed on July 18, 2017.

UN 2375. (2017). *Resolution 2375 North Korea.* http://www.un.org/en/ga/search/view_doc.asp?symbol=S/RES/2375(2017). Accessed on September 26, 2017.

Weaver, John M. (2017). Cyber Threats to the National Security of the United States: A Qualitative Assessment (Chapter). In *Focus on Terrorism (Volume 15).* Nova Science Publishers, New York [(Joshua Morgan (editor)].

WEF. (2018). The Global Risks Report 2018 (13th Edition). *World Economic Forum.* http://www3.weforum.org/docs/WEF_GRR18_Report.pdf. Accessed on January 19, 2018.

WTA. (2017). *Worldwide Threat Assessment.* https://www.dni.gov/files/documents/Newsroom/Testimonies/SSCI%20Unclassified%20SFR%20-%20Final.pdf. Accessed on January 20, 2018.

· 8 ·

UNITED KINGDOM

History and Background of the U.K.

The United Kingdom (U.K.) has a rich history and maintained a position as a significant global power from the 18th century until the end of World War II (Tombs, 2015). The UK has historically played a prominent role in developing parliamentary democracy and in advancing both science and literature (CIA, 2018). At its pinnacle in the 19th century, the British Empire extended its reach over 25% of the earth's surface (Tombs, 2015). Its decline began in the first half of the 20th century as the U.K.'s strength seriously atrophied in the wake of two world wars and the Irish Republic's withdrawal from the union (Tombs, 2015). The second half of the 20th century witnessed the dismantling of its Empire and the move on its part to rebuild itself into a modern and prosperous nation in Europe. As one of five permanent members of the U.N. Security Council, a founding member of the North Atlantic Treaty Organization (NATO), and the Commonwealth, the U.K. still pursues a global approach to foreign policy (CIA, 2018).

The U.K. has been an integral member of the EU since its accession in 1973, although it chose to remain outside the Economic and Monetary Union. That stated in June of 2016 amid frustration with its perception of the

EU bureaucracy in Brussels compounded by massive migration into the country, U.K. citizens exercised their vote and opted to leave the EU (CIA, 2018). Presently, the U.K. and the EU are currently negotiating the terms of the U.K.'s withdrawal; they will move forward with discussions on a framework for their future relationship ahead of the U.K.'s scheduled departure from the EU in March of 2019 (CIA, 2018).

The government of the U.K. is a parliamentary constitutional monarchy (Turpin & Tompkins, 2011). It consists of different parties (Mandelson & Liddle, 1996; Pugh, 2011). Its executive branch has a chief of state; Queen Elizabeth II has occupied this position since 1952. The head of government is Prime Minister Theresa May and she has been in power since July 2016. The cabinet of the U.K. is appointed by the prime minister. The monarchy is a right of lineage (hereditary) and usually, the leader of the majority party or majority coalition ends up becoming the Prime Minister (Jefferys, 2007).

The legislative branch of the U.K. is a bicameral Parliament and is comprised of the House of Lords (membership not fixed and since December 2016, 809 lords have been eligible to participate in the government's work—692 of these as life peers, 91 are hereditary peers, and 26 are clergy). The monarch appoints members on the advice of the prime minister and non-party political members are recommended by the House of Lords Appointments Commission (Turpin & Tompkins, 2011). Conversely, the House of Commons has 650 seats; the House of Commons membership is directly elected in single-seat constituencies by a simple majority popular vote and members usually serve five year terms (CIA, 2018).

The U.K.'s judicial branch consists of a Supreme Court (with 12 justices including the court president and deputy president); it was created by the Constitutional Reform Act 2005 and subsequently implemented in October 2009 (Turpin & Tompkins, 2011). The judicial candidates are selected by an independent committee comprised of several judicial commissions and is followed by their recommendations to the prime minister; appointments are made by the monarch (Jefferys, 2007). Justices are appointed for life. Subordinate courts include England and Wales—the Court of Appeal (civil and criminal divisions); the High Court; County Courts; the Crown Court; the Magistrates' Courts; Sheriff Courts; Scotland—Court of Sessions; the High Court of Justiciary; tribunals; Northern Ireland—Court of Appeal in Northern Ireland; the High Court; county courts; magistrates' courts; and specialized tribunals (Turpin & Tompkins, 2011).

Militarily, the U.K. has historically expended over 2% of its gross domestic product on its defense establishment. Its armed forces include the Army, Royal Navy (includes Royal Marines), Royal Air Force (Tombs, 2015).

Dating back to 2002, Gibraltar residents through referendum voted overwhelmingly to reject any "shared sovereignty" arrangement between the U.K. and Spain (CIA, 2018). The Government of Gibraltar had insisted on equal participation in talks between the two countries and Spain disapproved of plans by the U.K. to grant greater autonomy to Gibraltar (CIA, 2018).

Both Mauritius and Seychelles claim the Chagos Archipelago located in the British Indian Ocean Territory (CIA, 2018). Back in 2001, the former inhabitants of the archipelago, those evicted from 1967 to 1973, were granted U.K. citizenship and the right of return, followed by Orders in Council in 2004 that banned rehabitation (CIA, 2018). A High Court ruling ended up reversing the ban, a Court of Appeal refused to hear the case, and what ensued was a Law Lords' decision in 2008 that denied the right of return (CIA, 2018).

Other territorial disputes include the Falkland Islands (Islas Malvinas) the South Sandwich Islands and South Georgia; a territorial claim in Antarctica (British Antarctic Territory) overlaps Argentine claim and partially overlaps a claim by Chile (CIA, 2018). Finally, Iceland, Ireland, and the U.K. dispute Denmark's claim that the Faroe Islands' continental shelf extends beyond 200 nautical miles (CIA, 2018).

U.K. Intelligence

The United Kingdom has potent intelligence capability. As mentioned in the chapter on France, Jalalzai (2016, p. 18) also considers this nation as one of four countries that have a formidable intelligence apparatus that is both powerful and influential within Europe. Like the French, the intelligence services of the United Kingdom are considered both professional and strong and is very capable at collection (Jalalzai, 2016, p. 9). Stemming in part from its role as a colonial ruler, it still has extensive capabilities the world over.

It has three main intelligence components. These include Military Intelligence Section Five (MI5), Military Intelligence Section Six (MI6), and the Government Communications Headquarters (GCHQ) (Lowenthal, 2017).

MI5 provides the Kingdom with domestic intelligence support and consists of approximately 4,000 personnel (Lowenthal, 2017). Its function encapsulates such roles as providing it with security against a myriad of threats that include those from terrorism, weapons of mass destruction (WMD), espionage, economic security threats, and cyber, and it is responsible for providing intelligence support to law enforcement (Lowenthal, 2017).

MI6 the U.K.'s intelligence organization charged with collection efforts by way of both human intelligence (HUMINT) and technical intelligence (TECHINT), subsequently produces finished intelligence products stemming from information gathered abroad (Lowenthal, 2017). It falls under the control of the Kingdom's foreign secretary (Lowenthal, 2017). According to a 2010 report, MI6 has just over 2,200 officers (Lowenthal, 2017).

Conversely, GCHQ is the purveyor of signals intelligence (SIGINT) for the United Kingdom. It, too, operates under the control of the foreign secretary and shares a close relationship with the National Security Agency of the United States (Lowenthal, 2017). Its staff is comprised of just about 5,800 personnel (Lowenthal, 2017).

Analysis of the U.K.

In terms of numbers of people, the United Kingdom comes in at number 22 overall in the world (just under France) and is the smallest in terms of numbers relative to the other four permanent members of the Security Council (UN, 2014). The U.K.'s GDP value is 2.5 trillion, placing it 5th in the world and in the middle nominally when looking at the five permanent Security Council members.

The rest of this section is dedicated to the application of the YIRTM-M and how it applies to United Kingdom. Supporting data for this section is found in Annex 8.1. Here one will find the exact breakdown by instruments for the data supporting the analysis section. Likewise, the variation of sources tied back to the Federal Secondary Data Case Study Triangulation Model will also show the balance in sources contributing to the analysis of each instrument of national power.

President Trump met privately with Prime Minister Theresa May at the 2017 G20 conference. While meeting, the two leaders discussed the importance of a range of issues that included trade, counterterrorism and foreign policy (White House Press Release, 2017). During a recent meeting of the U.N. Security Council, the U.K. supported President Trump's call for greater sanctions regarding recent nuclear and ballistic missile tests by North Korea showing support for U.S. initiatives leading to stronger and more meaningful sanctions regarding North Korea's tests. May even stressed the importance of enhanced foreign relations with the United States at a meeting with Trump in September 2017 (May, 2017).

Like France, the United Kingdom's electoral system makes use of paper ballots (Electoral Commission, 2017). It too, is concerned about foreign influence in future elections.

The United Kingdom has an extensive network for acquiring information and by extension intelligence. It has effectively used ties to its colonial past (similar to France) to leverage intelligence for its personal benefit in modern times (Honig & Zimskind, 2017, p. 432).

Like one has seen in other countries, technology and information can be seen as a way to improve a country's position. Conversely, overreliance on it presents a case for exposing vulnerabilities (Clark, 2017, p. 31). What's more is that this country's infrastructure is vulnerable to adversaries exploiting network weaknesses in particular with regards to national infrastructure (Clark, 2017, p. 31). Cyber threats are a mainstay concern (Clark, 2017, p. 21). To mitigate effects from CNO, CNE, and CNA, the U.K. has implemented its National Cyber Security Strategy 2016 to 2021 (Clark, 2017, p. 22). It has aspirations to become one of the most secure places in the world for the conduct of business over the Internet. It is committed to a public-private partnership to strengthen its cyber resiliency (Cyber, 2017, p. 1).

While staying on the information component, the United Kingdom has engaged with the U.S. bilaterally on cyber security (DOS, 2016, p. 10). This is in an effort to strengthen alliances among like-minded nations in relation to government activities, civil groups, and private sector entities.

Militarily, the United Kingdom is looking to its national interests over those of collective alliance partners (McCormack, 2015). The U.K. has made inroads into its security and preservation over traditional Cold War venues though McCormack (2015) argues that it could be at the detriment to the country. Yet the U.K. still experiences acts of terror on its soil like the recent bombing in London on September 13 of 2017 (Trump, 2017). When looking at contemporary threats, estimates show that 85 terror groups operate throughout the United Kingdom (Jalalzai, 2016, p. 20). Both the U.K. and U.S. stressed recently the need for maintaining strong security and defense relations (May, 2017).

The U.K. acknowledges that terrorism and the instability and extremism that ensue from attacks is a foremost concern for its security (Clark, 2017, p. 21). That stated, it has extensive experience in dealing with acts of terror and in the implementation of anti-terrorism legislation (Alati, 2015, p. 97). These have increased in complexity, diversity and scale. To help reduce the threat of transnational terrorism to exact damage on Great Britain and its territorial interests, it has implemented a counterterrorism strategy referred to as CONTEST as a risk reduction effort (Clark, 2017, p. 22). The four principles that underpin CONTEST include prevent, pursue, protect and prepare.

It sees the utility in the U.N. Security Council to help it achieve its ends. More specifically, it has entered into bilateral discussion on the topic of extremism and terror with China and Russia as well as the U.S. (DOS 2, 2017).

The U.K. clearly sees terrorism as a key problem. In a period of waning budgets and fiscal constraints, it has increased resource availability to counter terror operations in 2016 (DOS2, 2017). Recent attacks in the U.K. have called into question whether or not security measures utilized by the United Kingdom are adequate (Jalalzai, 2016, p. 18).

Likewise, its efforts have taken it to the Middle East to conduct counter ISIS operations in both Syria and Iraq, to Africa to fight the Islamic State in Libya, and even through better information sharing throughout the EU; it has also upped its game to counter terror financing (DOS2, 2017). The U.K. is also still operating in Afghanistan to combat Daesh (MOD, 2017, p. 11).

Economics is at the epicenter to the U.K.'s security interests (Cormack, 2014). Cormack (2014) writes on the linkages of traditional concepts gravitating around political-military security and national interests and the interdependence of intelligence and security actors. Theresa May also confirmed her support to expanding trade during a bilateral meeting with President Trump during the 72nd Session of the U.N. General Assembly (May, 2017).

Early in its 2017 in *National Security and Infrastructure Investment Review*, the U.K.'s Department for Business, Energy & Industrial Strategy, Greg Clark (2017, p. 2) understands the inextricable linkage of economic interests to the national security. Moreover, he sees the clarity, consistency and proportionally of the two as being codependent for prosperity and viability. This report goes on to show that shared economic interests with other countries is a way for the United Kingdom to build and enhance its security interests. Another vulnerability that the U.K. realizes is foreign ownership of its companies (Clark, 2017, p. 21). These threats have increased significantly since the country's last assessment that dates to 2010.

As the United Kingdom moves forward, it is concerned with a triad of concerns. These include the likes of protecting its people, exerting global influence, and promoting prosperity (Clark, 2017, p. 21).

Implications for Intelligence Professionals

The United Kingdom will find itself in a challenging environment as it extricates itself from the European Union. Intelligence professionals will likely see the U.K. aggressively using diplomacy as a way to seek out new arrangements that will financially benefit the Kingdom. This is particularly true with the relationship growing between the U.S. and U.K. in 2017 and early 2018. It will not want to see slippage in its ranking (5th in the world in terms of GDP) and for the U.K. to be seen as a strong power will have to leverage its economic position to remain relevant. Its diplomats will likely pursue U.N. efforts that gravitate around inhibiting nation states looking to pursue and/or use weapons of mass destruction like the countries of Iran, North Korea, and Syria.

The U.K. has experienced network attacks in recent years, understands its vulnerabilities, and is planning accordingly. As is seen through the Cyber Security Strategy 2016 to 2021, the intelligence services will see that its CND efforts will improve and it appears committed to mitigate the threats to vulnerabilities from adversarial CNA and CNE attempts. Its GCHQ will be instrumental in its cyber improvements. The Kingdom historically has had close ties to the United States' National Security Agency and will continue to leverage this relationship to help look for cyber threats (as well as other none-computer related ones). It will likely continue a strong intelligence sharing relationship with the United States more generally, and when dealing with issues pertaining to terrorism, and will likely share information with other allies like France. While remaining on the topic of terror, one will likely see the U.K. support UNSC measures aimed at hurting those using terrorism to advance their causes (like Iran).

It will look to use its military, like France, to target Islamic extremists in countries outside of its border to weaken them so that they won't be able to orchestrate attacks from abroad within its own borders. The U.K.'s intelligence services will be instrumental in assisting the military in its conduct of threat assessments. Intelligence professionals will likely see the Kingdom use its military to support allies (and leverage the synergies achieved by coalition efforts) in order to weaken threats. It would like to also realize greater legitimacy in support from the United Nations as it looks to pursue military targets abroad.

Economically, and segueing from diplomacy, intelligence professionals will likely find the U.K. doubling down on efforts to enter into trade agreements especially as it pursues greater autonomy from exiting the European Union. Likewise, it will remain apprehensive of foreign acquisition of its companies and will want to hedge against foreign influence stemming from such business arrangements. Though it is interested in improving its economic interests, it will likely avoid agreements that will allow other countries to have agreements in place that could weaken its private job sector at home.

Annex 8.1 U.K.

How/Why	D.I.M.E.	Author(s)	Source Type	Date	Page
Trade, counterterrorism and foreign policy	D, M, E	White House Press Release	Press Release	2017	NA
Electoral system makes use of paper ballet but social media still vulnerable	I	Electoral Commission	System	2017	NA
Militarily, the United Kingdom is looking to its national interests over those of collective alliance partners (McCormack 2015); The UK has made inroads to its security and preservation over traditional Cold War venues though McCormack (2015) argues could be at the detriment to the country	D, M	McCormack	Journal	2015	
Economics is at the epicenter to the UK's security interests (Cormack 2015); it relies on the linkages of traditional concepts gravitating around political-military security and national interests and the interdependence of intelligence and security actors	E	Cormac	Journal	2014	

How/Why	D.I.M.E.	Author(s)	Source Type	Date	Page
The United Kingdom has an extensive network for acquiring information and by extension intelligence; it has effectively used ties to its colonial past (similar to France) to leverage intelligence for its personal benefit in modern times	I	Honig & Zimskind	Journal	2017	432
UK supported President Trump's call for greater sanctions regarding recent nuclear and ballistic missile tests by North Korea country showing support for U.S. initiatives leading to greater sanctions regarding North Korea's tests	D	UN2375	Government Document	2017	NP
Confirmed interests in expanding bilateral trade during a bilateral meeting with President Trump during the 72nd Session of the U.N. General Assembly	E	May	Press Release	2017	NP
May stressed the importance of shared foreign relations with the United States at a meeting with Trump in September 2017	D	May	Press Release	2017	NP
Both the U.K. and U.S. stressed the need for maintaining strong security and defense relations	M	May	Press Release	2017	NP
The United Kingdom has engaged with the U.S. bilaterally on cyber security	I, E	DOS	Government Document	2016	10
The U.K. has entered into bilateral discussion on the topic of extremism and terror with both China and Russia as well as the U.S.	D, M	DOS2	Government Document	2017	72

How/Why	D.I.M.E.	Author(s)	Source Type	Date	Page
It has increased resource availability to counter terror operations in 2016	M, E	DOS2	Government Document	2017	166
U.K. efforts have taken it to the Middle East to conduct counter ISIS operations in both Syria and Iraq, to Africa to fight the Islamic State in Libya, and even through better information sharing throughout the E.U.; it has also upped its game to counter terror financing	D, I, M, E	DOS2	Government Document	2017	166
The U.K. has extensive experience in dealing with acts of terror and in the implementation of anti-terrorism legislation	D, M	Alati	Journal	2015	97
It is also still operating in Afghanistan to combat Daesh	M	MOD	Government Document	2017	11
It is committed to a public-private partnership to strengthen its cyber resiliency	I	Cyber	Government Document	2017	1
Overreliance on information technology presents a case for exposing vulnerabilities	I	Clark	Government Document	2017	31
Inextricable linkage of economic interests to the national security	E	Clark	Government Document	2017	2
Infrastructure vulnerability to cyber	E	Clark	Government Document	2017	31
Mitigate effects from CNO, CNE, and CNA	E, I	Clark	Government Document	2017	22
Aspirations to become one of the most secure places in the world for the conduct of business over the Internet	E, I	Clark	Government Document	2017	22

How/Why	D.I.M.E.	Author(s)	Source Type	Date	Page
Implemented a counterter-rorism strategy referred to as CONTEST as a risk reduction effort; the four principles that underpin CONTEST include prevent, pursue, protect and prepare	M	Clark	Government Document	2017	22

References

Alati, Daniel. (2015). Current National Security and Human Rights Issues in the United Kingdom, Canada, and Hong Kong. *ILSA Journal of International & Comparative Law.* 22(1): 91.

CIA. (2018). *United Kingdom.* https://www.cia.gov/library/publications/resources/the-world-factbook/geos/uk.html. Accessed on April 20, 2018.

Clark, Greg. (2017). *National Security and Infrastructure Investment Review.* Department for Business, Energy & Industrial Strategy. https://www.gov.uk/government/consultations/national-security-and-infrastructure-investment-review. Accessed on October 17, 2017.

Cormack, Rory. (2014). Secret Intelligence and Economic Security: The Exploitation of a Critical Asset. *Intelligence and National Security.* 29(1): 99–121.

Cyber. (2017). *Defence Cyber Protection Partnership.* file:///C:/Users/email/Desktop/todo/8.pdf. Accessed on October 18, 2017.

DOS. (2016). *Department of State International Cyberspace Policy Strategy Public Law 114–113.* file:///C:/Users/email/AppData/Local/Microsoft/Windows/INetCache/IE/2VY0JPMC/255732.pdf. Accessed on October 17, 2017.

DOS2. (2017). Country Reports on Terrorism 2016. *Department of State.* https://www.state.gov/j/ct/rls/crt/2016/index.htm. Accessed on October 17, 2017.

Electoral Commission. (2017). *The Electoral Commission.* https://www.electoralcommission.org.uk/our-work/roles-and-responsibilities/our-role-in-elections-and-referendums. Accessed on July 23, 2017.

Honig, Or and Sarah Zimskind. (2017). The Spy Machine and the Ballot Box: Examining Democracy's Intelligence Advantage. *International Journal of Intelligence and Counterintelligence.* 3(3): 431–463.

Jalalzai, Musa Khan. (2016). *Fixing the EU Intel Crisis: Intelligence Sharing, Law Enforcement, and the Threat of Chemical Biological, and Nuclear Terrorism.* Algora Publishing.

Jefferys, Kevin. (2007). *Politics and the People: A History of British Democracy Since 1918.* Atlantic.

Lowenthal, Mark M. (2017). *Intelligence from Secrets to Policy* (7th Edition). Sage Press.

Mandelson, Peter and Roger Liddle. (1996). *The Blair Revolution: Can New Labour Deliver.* Faber.

May, Theresa. (2017). *Remarks by President Trump and Prime Minister May of the United Kingdom Before Bilateral Meeting.* https://www.whitehouse.gov/the-press-office/2017/09/20/remarks-president-trump-and-prime-minister-may-united-kingdom-bilateral. Accessed on September 26, 2017.

McCormack, Tara. (2015). The British National Security Strategy: Security After Representation. *The British Journal of Politics and International Relations.* 17(3): 494–511.

MOD. (2017). *Finance & Economic Annual Bulletin Departmental Resources Statistics 2016.* https://www.gov.uk/government/uploads/system/uploads/attachment_data/file/580469/Commentary_relating_to_Finance___Economics_Annual_Statistical_Bulletin___Departmental_Resources___January_2017.pdf. Accessed on October 17, 2017.

Pugh, Martin. (2011). *Speak for Britain: A New History of the Labour Party.* Vintage Press.

Tombs, Robert. (2015). *The English and Their History.* New York: Alfred A. Knopf.

Trump, Donald. (2017). *Remarks by the President on the London Terror Bombing.* https://www.whitehouse.gov/the-press-office/2017/09/15/remarks-president-london-terror-bombing. Accessed on September 26, 2017.

Turpin, Colin and Adam Tompkins. (2011). *British Government and the Constitution.* Cambridge University Press.

UN. (2014). *UN Data a World of Information.* http://data.un.org/Data.aspx?d=POP&f=tableCode%3a1. Accessed on July 18, 2017.

UN2375. (2018). United Nations Security Resolutions 2375. http://unscr.com/en/resolutions/2375. Accessed on April 18, 2018.

White House Press Release 4. (2017). *Readout of President Donald J. Trump's Meeting with Prime Minister Theresa May of the United Kingdom.* https://www.whitehouse.gov/the-press-office/2017/07/08/readout-president-donald-j-trumps-meeting-prime-minister-theresa-may. Accessed on July 18, 2017.

· 9 ·

ANALYSIS AND FINDINGS

The U.S. in particular, should be concerned about what is taking place and realistically, what it needs to do to remain the dominant world power. Specifically, this is true in the context in the continual growth of this nation's deficit spending and its debt. Regarding the deficit, it has grown to $587 billion up by 33% from just the year before (GAO 17-579T, 2017). Moreover, the debt as a share of the gross domestic product also rose by 3% (to 77%) from fiscal year 2015 to 2016 (GAO-17 579T, 2017). The U.S. debt as of early 2018 is well over $20 trillion and those in the IC of the U.S. should see this as a significant challenge moving forward.

That stated, true leadership is what can serve as a catalyst for positive change. The threat to peace and stability remain throughout the world and is real (Weaver, 2015). Inextricable linkage among the nation states throughout the planet and by extension through globalization could have an impact on the stability of the world economy. More to the point, it will become progressively important to nurture and grow relationships with other international partners with particular attention afforded to those in the intelligence profession (those that are friendly to the United States and even those with whom it doesn't always share an enduring friendship), fostering greater peace and security around the globe.

This should be done while striving to make the world a less dangerous place. A utilitarian approach pursued by intelligence leaders should look beyond their field of expertise whether it is country focused, regionally oriented, or functional aligned (i.e. terrorism, proliferation, narcotics, etc.) and eye what outcomes their decision will have holistically to ensure that greater damage is not done while pushing for short term gains within one's narrow purview (Weaver, 2018).

Q1: How are the permanent members of the Security Council of the United Nations using the instruments of national power to shape outcomes favorable to them?

Diplomatically, the nations will pursue measures to help increase their prominence in the world. Likewise, they will continue to foster relations with countries that are aligned culturally with their ways and will strengthen relations in order to do so. Those working as professionals in the intelligence field should see the connection of diplomacy in all facets of activity carried out by a country.

Information is a key to helping garner support. Russia will most likely use its influences and adeptness in social media to help shift elections where possible to lend support to politicians who have leanings towards it. Russia and China will most likely make use of cyber as a way to continue to steal trade secrets, proprietary information, and military blueprints to help reduce research and development costs while also undercutting the technical superiority possessed through systems owned and utilized by France, the United Kingdom, and the United States. All countries are moving in a direction that will tighten CND in an effort to mitigate the effects from other countries into future election cycles. Intelligence analysts should constantly strive to figure out what the outcomes or effects that a nation wants to achieve by pursuing cyber activities and to gain insight into the capabilities that one wants to achiever whether it is for CNA, CNE, and/or CND.

Militarily, Russia and China will most likely increase expenditures relative to their gross domestic product to exert greater influence with Russia's being limited regionally and China's expanding more globally. Conversely, France and the United Kingdom will either maintain or only make modest increases due to economic hardships experienced through the recent European recession despite for calls by the United States for NATO nations to increase spending on defense. That stated, strength of the power possessed by France, the U.K., and the U.S. can be further complemented by their participation in NATO. Militarily, those working in intelligence should see whether or not France and the U.K. will want to expand or contract in terms of contributions to NATO and to see the specific capabilities being pursued by China and Russia all to gain greater insight into the direction of the armed forces of these four countries.

One thing is certain; all nations are against the Islamic State. This is evident through the approval of U.N. Security Resolution 2379 on September 21st, 2017 (UN2379, 2017). Here, all five nations are in concurrence that terrorism is bad and see nothing favorable coming out of the proliferation of this terror group.

Finally, China will most likely try to fill the vacuum left by the United States pulling out of the Trans Pacific Partnership to not only enhance its economic standing but as a way to invest in its military buildup. Russia can use weapons sales as a way to provide it with hard currency and it can leverage petroleum shipments to many of the Eastern European countries to hedge against NATO influences in the region. Economically, Europe will have to properly prepare for the U.K.'s departure from the European Union so as to not adversely move the continent back to recession.

Intelligence professionals would be wise to monitor the European Union. They should see how the withdrawal of the U.K. from the union will impact both the E.U. more broadly, and the United Kingdom more specifically.

When turning to China, intelligence analysts should look at the indicators of trading alliances, economic growth, leadership to fill the TPP vacuum, and where this country is establishing economic ties in future years. Likewise, they should gain granularity into capital investment projects leading to the pursuit of advanced weapon systems.

Russia is a unique challenge to those that work in the intelligence community. Its economic viability will be interlinked broadly on the global commodities' market and more specifically on the pricing of gas and oil. Intelligence professionals should monitor weapons exports and sales (and the specific consumers of these products) to gain insight into those nations with whom they might building a stronger relationship.

Q2: Why are the permanent members of the Security Council of the United Nations using the instruments of national power to shape outcomes favorable to them?

Permanent members of the UNSC at times will see utility in sharing information with one or more members for the advancement of their own security interests. Diplomatic efforts can help maintain alliances. All countries would like to either maintain or rise in prominence and will attempt to use their diplomatic efforts broadly to do so, and more specifically will utilize their position as permanent security members (and the threat of veto) to shore up their positions.

The permanent members will use information to help shape public perceptions to better promote their image (and by extension their influence). Likewise, they will invest in efforts to protect against propaganda and other adverse influences exerted by state and non-state actor CNA and CNE efforts to prevent them from succumbing to exploitation. Intelligence professionals should monitor these countries' efforts to see if they are effective at preventing or at least minimizing nefarious intrusions of those purveying cyber as a tool to implement information operations (with the intent of influencing elections as a primary example).

Investment will continue in their militaries with likely increases in those of China and Russia and maintenance of capabilities in France and the United Kingdom. The former two will do so to leverage greater influence and power with the latter two focusing on leveraging capabilities from alliances like NATO. Strength is often equated to power which underscores the relevancy of this instrument to the four permanent Security Council members. Intelligence analysts can gain insightful perspectives into a country's direction by looking at the types of weapons systems being purchased by them (defensive vs. offensive), and the global garrisoning of a country's military members and capabilities.

Economically, China will likely use its position as the second largest economy to grow and to fill vacuums left by the U.S. retracting its economic influence abroad (through backing out of such agreements as the TPP). Russia, would like to continue to grow its economy and most notably can through the export of petroleum products, metals, and weapons provided that it sees an easing of sanctions levied against it. France, through the exit of the U.K. from the European Union, would like to assume a leadership role alongside Germany, through divorcing itself of the financial burdens linked to the EU and wants to grow its economy through bilateral agreements.

Under economic issues, intelligence professional should conduct deep analysis into the financial interests of a particular country, the implementation one's trade agreements, and the growth relatively (or contraction thereof) of its GDP over time and more. This will give insight as to whether a country is gaining or losing prominence from a monetary perspective.

Q3: What are the implications for the United States?

The information instrument as used by other UNSC members is the most immediate concern for the United States. Information as an instrument of national power has implications among the four other permanent members of the Security Council of the United Nations. Most notably, China and Russia will most likely remain major users of cyber as a way to weaken the United States and by extension its two main allies, France and the United Kingdom, and this has been underscored by a recent economic report showing an increase in recent years of state-on-state cyber attacks (WEF, 2018, p. 33). What's more is that these CNOs have increased exponentially in recent years. Russia and China according to the secondary sources seemingly have been engaged in cyber espionage activities the world over (Weaver, 2017).

Cyber continues to be a major vulnerability for this country particularly. Accordingly, the United States must invest in greater cybersecurity (especially at the federal government level) to have more effective and robust TTPs to mitigate exposure from vulnerabilities (GAO 17-533, 2017). France and the U.K. should too, as well as other developed nations allied with the United States. This is in light that cyber threats are likely to grow in sophistication and number. Most notably, the nation can expect more of the same from China and Russia (GAO 17-533, 2017). Moreover, what is necessary is the implementation of improved TTPs to detect, respond, and mitigate from cyber threats (GAO 17-440T, 2017). What's more is the necessity to invest in strengthening the cybersecurity of the critical infrastructure of the nation as a whole (GAO 17-440T, 2017). Most notably, China and Russia will likely remain major purveyors of cyber as a way to weaken France, the United Kingdom, and the United States. The three of the latter must build redundancies to protect themselves while knowing that the two former will try to use these to advance their positions and stature on the world stage. Intelligence analysts should always monitor cyber and information activities pursued by a country.

The U.S. has prided itself on being a technological leader in the world, but a recent Government Accountability Office document underscored the challenges confronting the U.S. in the cyber domain particularly with a need to mitigate cyberspace threats and the necessity to enhance these capabilities (GAO 17-369, 2017).

Globalization has made the world a more complex place. Nation states could see themselves aligned on one matter and yet they could be diametrically opposed to the same country or countries on other issues. The members of the United States' IC (military and civilian) and those of her enduring long-term friends, must come to terms with this new reality and could use the

"D.I.M.E." approach to help gain granularity regarding the situation as they look at potential impacts of their decisions on relationships among the countries with whom interaction occurs and globalization more generally especially in the context of relations among the United Nations Security Council's permanent members. Likewise, it would behoove the IC to develop an appreciation for what is going on with the targeted country that moves beyond their specific country or region, if their organizations are geographically arrayed.

Regarding this research, the YIRTM-M was useful too in conducting the analysis. Each instrument of national power was considered in the context of the four other permanent members of the Security Council. Subsequently, data from the chapter annexes was used underscoring evidence for each country. Figure 9.1 shows a gradation of the instruments as used by the four other permanent members (the darker, the more the instrument was used).

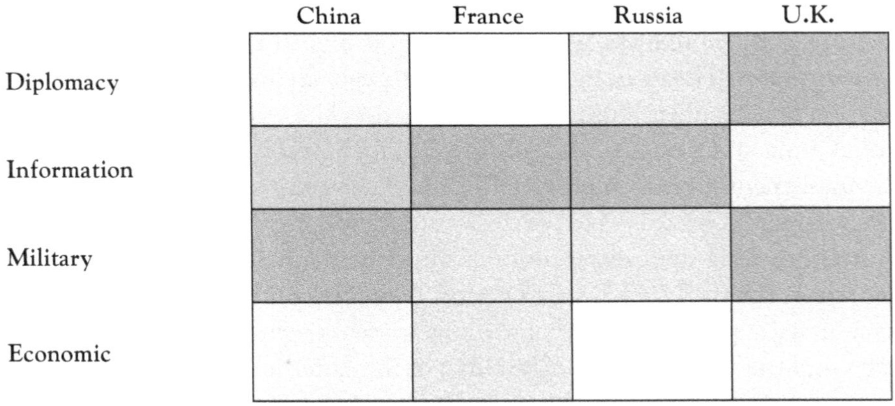

Figure 9.1. Instruments of national power as used by China, France, Russia and the United Kingdom

China is a significant trading partner with the United States and a nation whose economy is burgeoning with each passing year. It sees its economic growth as being directly linked to national security and has leveraged information technology as a way to reduce the technological edge the United States holds by engaging in cyber espionage. At present, it too realizes that it can't confront the United States in a direct military operation and win and has also invested in cyber offensive capabilities to look for vulnerabilities in the infrastructure and defense sectors of the United States. That stated, China continues to invest heavily in its military modernization especially in capabilities that provide it reach beyond the confines of Asia. Diplomatic efforts are linked to economic initiatives to help grow China's position. It has used its position as a member of the Security Council to serve as a counterbalance to the United States thereby weakening its influence.

France is a key ally of the United States and a powerful member of NATO. Accordingly, it has made use of the information instrument of power to protect against cyber threats, fostered network defense and used information and intelligence sharing (both as a contributor and recipient) to thwart attacks and go after those bent on harming it. Economic pursuits were utilized to enhance diplomatic and military efforts. Likewise, it has implemented diplomatic efforts and military power to exert influence, shore up alliances, and pursue those actors (most notably those engaged in terror tactics) to fight them outside of Europe.

Russia, since the fall of communism in the early 1990s has fallen in and out of favor numerous times with the United States. Though it has seemingly become more assertive in recent years, it still falls behind the other three permanent members in this study in terms of economic position but has invested heavily in its military capabilities. That stated, it realizes that it can't match the United States and NATO allies militarily and accordingly has invested in cyber (information) as an asymmetric TTP. When turning to the military instrument of national power, Russia has invested in and extensively used this to show the world that it has the ability and willingness to conduct operations in both Europe and the Middle East. Diplomatic efforts are used in conjunction with information as a way to try to convince the world that what it is doing is right. Diplomatically, it has also used its position as a member of the Security Council to exert influence over the United States to help marginalize its position at times.

The United Kingdom, like France, has been a strong supporter of the United States and a significant member of the NATO alliance. It particularly focused on diplomatic and military efforts as a way to hold onto power. Following these two instruments, the U.K. looked at the application of information as a way to promote its messaging while looking at ways to invest in cyber defense to guard against vulnerabilities that nefarious types could exploit. Economic means were also used but at a lesser extent than the other three.

The United Nations is still relevant though. As was the case leading to the cessation to Iran's nuclear enrichment program through the implementation of the Joint Comprehensive Plan of Action in the summer of 2015; indications show that the P5 members are in step with countering North Korea from pursuing a nuclear ballistic missile program, to keep nuclear weapons out of Northeast Asia to hopefully lead to greater regional stability in Northeast Asia.

A study on the United Kingdom and other members of the European community underscores challenges emanating from terrorism (Maftei, 2015). Europe has experienced a significant increase in terror incidents; the United Kingdom and France are no exceptions. Both of these two permanent Security Council members have shouldered the brunt of many of these attacks. Accordingly, these two countries in particular will be interested in fomenting relations through diplomacy and militarily to hopefully prevent future acts of terror or extremism and militarily will contribute where possible to help weaken the Islamic State in places like Iraq and Syria.

More specifically, the United Nations Security Council is still a relevant and powerful organization. Accordingly, those that make up the permanent members have significant influence in determining what resolutions proceed. The degree to which intelligence is shared between or among these actors could be determined in part by what Walsh (2012, p. 137) refers to as a hierarchy. More specifically, as nations within these five see the inextricable linkage of security and economic growth to one another, those could have an impact on the degree to which they will be willing to work with one another. That stated, intelligence could be seen as an integral component to the fields of foreign policy and international relations (Walsh, 2012). Professionals from the intelligence fields the world over in general, and the intelligence community members of the United States more specifically, could benefit from understanding the inter connectedness of the United Nations Security Council's permanent members. Intelligence professionals should periodically revisit the National Security Strategy, the Joint Strategic Plan, and the National Defense Strategy to see how, when, and why the other permanent members are doing things that support or negate the United States' interests.

References

GAO 17-369. (2017). *Actions Needed to Address Five Key Mission Challenges.* http://www.gao.gov/products/gao-17-369. Accessed on July 23, 2017.

GAO 17-440T. (2017). *Cybersecurity: Actions Needed to Strengthen U.S. Capabilities.* http://www.gao.gov/assets/690/682756.pdf. Accessed on July 23, 2017.

GAO 17-533. (2017). *Cybersecurity: Federal Efforts Are Under Way That May Address Workforce Challenges.* http://www.gao.gov/assets/690/683923.pdf. Accessed on July 23, 2017.

GAO 17-579T. (2017). *The Nation's Fiscal Health: Actions Needed to Address the Federal Government's Fiscal Future*. http://www.gao.gov/products/GAO-17-579T. Accessed on July 23, 2017.

Maftei, Danut. (2015). The Way Several European Countries Use to Achieve Their Strategic and Security Objectives by Involving the National Experts Seconded to International Organizations: Case Study: United Kingdom and The Netherlands. *Journal of Criminal Investigations*. 8(1): 62–72.

UN 2379. (2017). *Resolution 2379 Islamic State*. http://www.un.org/en/ga/search/view_doc.asp?symbol=S/RES/2379(2017). Accessed on September 26, 2017.

Walsh, James. (2012). *The International Politics of Intelligence Sharing*. Columbia University Press.

Weaver, John M. (2015). The Perils of a Piecemeal Approach to Fighting ISIS in Iraq. *Public Administration Review*. 75(2): 192–193.

Weaver, John M. (2017). Cyber Threats to the National Security of the United States: A Qualitative Assessment (Chapter). In *Focus on Terrorism (Volume 15)*. Nova Science Publishers, New York [(Joshua Morgan (editor)].

Weaver, John M. (2018). Dissecting the 2017 National Security Strategy: Implications for Senior Administrators (the Devil in the Details). *Global Policy*. 9(2): 283–284.

WEF. (2018). The Global Risks Report 2018 (13th Edition). *World Economic Forum*. http://www3.weforum.org/docs/WEF_GRR18_Report.pdf. Accessed on January 19, 2018.

· 1 0 ·

CONCLUSION

The Federal Secondary Data Case Study Triangulation Model was useful to collect data on and help ensure balance in understanding regarding this study. Most of the evidence from this research came from the bottom left of the model (mostly written sources like government document, books, and journals). These sources provided the greatest insight into what is occurring with each of the four nations. Oral accounts from the bottom right contributed significantly to but to a lesser extent than the documents component. Press releases, key leader statements, and testimony helped complement what the written sources provided. Plans and systems were also useful in triangulation to help understand what is taking place. Figure 10.1 shows the breakout of data sources; the darker the color, the more that were used.

	China	France	Russia	UK
Plans & Systems (Assessments)				
Documents/Legislation/Policy/ (Journals/Reports)				
Press Releases/Testimony/ Interviews (Key Leaders)				

Figure 10.1 Sources of data

Here, one can see how the data are arrayed in relation to the Federal Secondary Data Case Study Triangulation Model and the YIRTM-M. Most of the evidence supporting the analysis and findings came from the documents/legislation/policy portion of the former model. The next highest frequency in evidence came from press releases/testimony/interview component of the former model. Plans and systems, accounted for the least amount of evidence regarding this study.

Future studies can continue to look at the relevance and importance of the permanent members of the United Nations Security Council. Likewise, future research could look to the modified YIRTM-M and Federal Secondary Data Case Study Triangulation Models to help make sense of what is occurring. Going beyond the YRITM-M, other studies can consider NATO's Model or the PMESII (political, military, economic, social, infrastructure, and information) to add two additional variables to the analysis. Other recommendations include seeking out more plans and systems (assessments) and more oral accounts through the pursuit of information derived from press releases, testimony, interviews and other statements by key leaders.

Other future research could look beyond the scope of the United Nations. Studies could also look more pointedly at NATO, the Organization for Security and Cooperation for Europe (OSCE), the Association of Southeast Asian Nations (ASEAN) and more. Likewise, one might consider more detailed case analysis for any of the specific nations covered in this study.

Primary data was not used in this study. Other endeavors to build on what this one found could include questionnaires, personal interviews, focus groups, and more to triangulate on results to confirm or refute what this study found.

When turning back to the intelligence community, things are not often as they appear. Those who conduct assessments and judgments for their nations need to understand the complexity in looking at relationships among different state actors. Though it is unlikely that assessments and judgments will be clear with straightforward information, intelligence professionals should strive to make sure things are as understandable as possible (Jervis, 2010, p. 203). It is through this understanding that those looking to provide products for consumption by those charged with a nation's security might be able to provide better assessments in developing foreign policy when looking to see just who are friends and foes.

Those that work in the intelligence community throughout the world would be well-served to afford consideration to how the UNSC permanent members will react to various foreign policy initiatives, military actions, and economic inducements, trade incentive, tariffs, embargos and more to see how the UNSC will likely act. Likewise, the actions set forth by the UNSC members could have unintended consequences for nations looking to exert their influence either regionally or globally especially when one or more countries from the P5 UNSC nations could be affected. Likewise, those intelligence professionals in the United States must look to predict what their political, military, and economic pursuits will have and how the other member nations might react to maintain their own status quo or take advantage of situations to enhance their own positions. Though the United States has a mixed record with regards to intelligence sharing with other agencies and even countries as a result of pressure from the White House and Congress, there are times when providing the information to others could lead to greater security (Walsh, 2012). Likewise, those within the UNSC should also consider reciprocation at times. This is especially true in the context of greater security throughout the world.

References

Jervis, Robert. (2010). Why Intelligence and Policymakers Clash. *Political Science Quarterly*. 125(2): 185–204.

Walsh, James. (2012). *The International Politics of Intelligence Sharing*. Columbia University Press, Columbia New York.

INDEX

A

Africa: 17, 22, 28, 40, 55, 56–57, 60, 82, 86
Air Force: 17, 34, 52, 79, 104
Analysis: 2, 8, 9, 13, 16–17, 19, 37–38, 53–54, 57, 67, 71, 80, 89, 91–95, 97, 100
Armed Forces: 17, 41, 53, 55, 65, 67, 79, 91
Army: 3, 9, 17, 34, 38–39, 44, 52, 79, 103
Asia: 4, 17, 27–28, 37, 40, 47, 66, 68, 70, 74, 94, 96, 100, 103

B

Background: 1, 11, 17, 33, 49, 63, 67, 77
Britain: 17, 82
Bureau: 17, 37, 41–42, 55, 67

C

C2: 17
C4ISR: 17, 31

China: 3–4, 8, 12, 17–18, 23, 26–28, 31, 33–46, 66, 68, 70–71, 75, 82, 85, 90–95, 100
CNA: 17, 39, 41, 43, 68, 73, 81, 83, 86, 90, 92
CND: 17, 39, 41, 45, 68, 71, 74, 83, 90, 90
CNE: 17, 39, 41, 43, 68, 73, 81, 83, 86, 90, 92
CNO: 17, 39, 41, 43, 81, 86, 93
CNR: 17, 52, 57
Congress: 17, 34, 101
Cyber: 3, 15, 17, 26, 31, 34, 36, 38–41, 43–45, 54, 58, 61, 68–74, 80–81, 83, 85–86, 90, 92–95
Cyberspace: 3, 17, 31, 93

D

Data: 3, 12–13, 15–16, 31, 37–38, 53, 54, 62, 67, 80, 94, 99–101
Defense: 17–18, 25, 26–31, 37–40, 42, 46, 51–54, 56, 58, 60, 65, 67, 69, 71, 73, 79, 81, 85, 90, 94–96, 103–104

DGSE: 17, 52–54, 57, 59
DGSI: 17, 53, 57
D.I.M.E.: 5, 15, 17, 42–46, 58–61, 73–74,
    84–87, 94
Diplomacy: 6, 13–14, 17, 27, 40, 83–84, 90,
    94, 96, 100
Diplomatic (Diplomat): 5–7, 17, 26, 28–29,
    38, 41–42, 45, 54, 56, 58, 67–70, 74,
    90–92, 94–95
DRM: 17, 53

E

Economy (Economic): 2–3, 5–8, 13, 15, 17,
    19, 21–22, 27–30, 33–35, 38–44, 49,
    51–53, 56–57, 60, 63–65, 70–73, 77,
    80, 82–84, 86, 89–96, 100–101
Espionage: 17, 36, 39–40, 42–44, 66, 69–71,
    73, 80, 93–94
Europe: 2, 3, 7, 17, 27, 37, 40–41, 56, 60,
    63, 77, 79, 91, 95–96, 100, 103
European Union: 1, 17, 30, 49, 54–55, 57,
    83–84
Evidence: 17, 39, 43, 70, 73, 94, 99–100

F

Federal Bureau of Investigation (FBI): 17, 55
Federal Secondary Data Case Study Triangu-
    lation Model: 31, 38, 54, 67, 80, 99–100
Finance: 17, 26, 31, 35, 51
France: 3, 8, 12, 14, 17, 22–23, 31, 49–61,
    71, 79–81, 83, 85, 90, 92–96, 100
FSB: 17, 66–68, 70

G

G7: 17
G8: 17
G20: 17, 38, 42, 80
GCHQ: 17, 79–80, 83
GDP: 17, 37, 42, 51–53, 65, 67, 80, 83, 92
Government: 1, 3, 13, 15, 17, 25–26, 28–29,
    33, 35, 37–39, 43, 45–46, 51, 57–61,
    64, 68, 70, 72–74, 78–79, 81, 85–87,
    93, 99, 103
Gross Domestic Product: 17, 34, 37, 51, 56,
    60, 79, 89–90
GRU: 17, 67–68, 71

H

Hard Power: 7, 17, 30
History: 17, 21, 33–34, 49, 63, 70, 77
Human Intelligence: 17, 53, 66, 80
HUMINT: 17, 53, 66, 80

I

Information: 1–6, 11–17, 26, 28, 37–41, 43,
    46, 52–55, 57, 59–60, 68–69, 71–72,
    74, 80–83, 85–86, 88, 90–95, 100–101
Intelligence: 1–7, 11–14, 17–18, 26, 31,
    36–42, 44, 52–57, 59, 61, 66–72, 74,
    79–85, 89–93. 95–96, 101
Intelligence Community (IC): 1–2, 5–8, 11,
    17, 41–42, 52, 54–56, 68–69, 89, 91,
    93–94, 96, 101
Interviews: 13, 16–17, 100–101
Iran: 2, 4–5, 17, 25, 27, 40, 66, 68, 72, 83, 95
Islamic State (ISIL and ISIS): 4–6, 17, 18,
    28–29, 56–57, 60, 82, 86, 91, 96

J

JCPOA: 18
Joint Comprehensive Plan of Action: 18, 95
Joint Security Plan (JSP): 18, 26, 28–30
Journal: 18, 43–45, 58–59, 73–74, 84–86, 99
Judicial (Judicial Branch): 18, 23, 29, 34,
    51, 64, 78

K

KGB: 18, 66
Korea: 4, 7, 18, 22, 25–28, 36, 38, 40, 45,
    54, 56–57, 59, 68, 74, 80–81, 83, 85, 95

M

Marine: 18, 34, 52, 79
MI5: 18, 79
MI6: 18, 79–80
Middle East: 18, 27, 30, 56, 60, 68, 74, 82, 86, 95, 103
Military: 18, 22, 27–31, 33–34, 36, 39–45, 49, 52–53, 55, 57–58, 63, 65–71, 73–74, 79, 82–84, 90–95, 100–101
Minister: 18, 50, 53, 55, 58, 64, 69, 73, 78, 80

N

National Defense Strategy (NDS): 18, 25, 27, 37, 67, 69, 96
NATO: 2–3, 18–19, 31, 49, 55–58, 69–72, 74, 77, 90–92, 95, 100, 103–104
Navy: 18, 34, 40, 44, 52, 65, 79
NSA: 18–19, 68–69
National Security Strategy (NSS): 18, 25–29, 31, 96

O

OSD: 18, 42–43

P

P5: 11–12, 16, 18, 95, 101
Parliament: 18, 49–50, 77–78
Permanent Members: 2, 6–8, 11–12, 15, 18, 23, 26, 69, 74, 77, 80, 90–96, 100–101
PLA: 18, 34
PLAAF: 18, 34
PLAN: 18, 34
Plans: 13, 18, 28, 39, 42–43, 79, 99–100
Power: 5–7, 11–15, 17–18, 22–23, 27–31, 36, 38, 51–52, 54, 56, 63, 67, 69, 71, 74, 77–80, 83, 89–96
Premier: 18, 33, 64
Press Release: 18, 99

R

Reconnaissance: 18, 31
Research: 11–13, 15–18, 39–41, 44, 90, 94, 99–100
Russia: 2–4, 8, 12, 18, 23, 27–28, 31, 36, 54–55, 58, 63–74, 82, 85, 90–95

S

Security: 2–3, 5, 8, 14, 18, 21–23, 26, 29–30, 34, 36– 37, 40, 45, 52, 54–56, 58, 66–67, 70, 79–82, 84–86, 89, 91–92, 94, 96, 101
Signals Intelligence (SIGINT): 18, 53, 66–67, 80
Soft Power: 18, 29–30
South China Sea (SCS): 4, 18, 27, 36–39, 42–44
Speech: 8, 13, 18, 39, 43, 72
Supreme Court: 18, 64, 78
Surveillance: 18, 31, 53–54, 59
SVR: 18, 66, 68, 70
Syria: 3–5, 18, 56–57, 60, 68, 70–72, 82–83, 86, 96
System: 13, 18–19, 26, 30–31, 33–35, 39, 41–44, 49, 55, 58, 69, 72–73, 81, 84, 90–92, 99–100

T

TECHINT: 19, 80
Terror (Terrorism): 8, 19, 21, 25–30, 53–58, 61, 80–83, 85–86, 90–91, 95–96
TPP: 19, 41–42, 91–92
TTP: 3, 14, 19, 38, 41, 68, 71, 93, 95
Testimony: 13, 18, 55, 58, 68, 72, 99–100

U

United Kingdom (UK): 3, 14, 18, 22–23, 31, 49, 54, 56–57, 60, 67, 71, 77, 79–85, 90–96, 100

United Nations (U.N.): 2–3, 5, 8, 11, 15, 18, 21–23, 26–28, 31, 37–39, 41–43, 45, 53, 56–57, 68, 71, 74, 77, 80, 82–85, 91, 95, 100

United Nations Security Council (UNSC): 6, 8, 11, 16, 18, 26, 41–42, 49, 57, 67, 71, 83, 91, 93–94, 96, 101

V

Vulnerability: 19, 82, 86, 93

W

Weapon Systems: 19, 30, 39, 42, 91

World Economic Forum (WEF): 19, 46

Worldwide Threat Assessment (WTA): 19, 38, 46

Y

York Intelligence Red Team Model – Modified (YIRTM–M): 11, 13–16, 31, 38, 54, 67, 80, 94, 100

ABOUT THE AUTHOR

John Michael Weaver is Assistant Professor of Intelligence Analysis at York College in Pennsylvania (USA), a retired DOD civilian from the United States' Intelligence Community and has served as an officer in the U.S. Army (retiring at the rank of lieutenant colonel). Since entering active duty, he has lived and worked on four continents and in nineteen countries spending nearly eight years overseas (working on behalf of the U.S. government). His experience includes multiple combat deployments, peace enforcement, peacekeeping, humanitarian relief and disaster assistance support in both conventional and unconventional/non-traditional units. In recent years, John has trained and certified multinational NATO reconnaissance teams based in The Netherlands, Germany and Spain for worldwide deployment to support full spectrum missions. He has also personally led several reconnaissance missions throughout Europe, the Middle East, and Asia (including multiple missions in Afghanistan); none of his team members have ever been injured or killed in the line of duty. He has received formal training/certification in the following areas from the U.S. Department of Defense: Survival/Evasion/Resistance/Escape (high risk), communications equipment and communications planning (FM radio, land line and satellite communications, encryption, and the use of cryptographic devices), digital camera use and digital photography courses, U.S. Joint Forces Command joint intelligence course, U.S. Special Operations Command counterintelligence awareness course (USSOCOM CI), U.S. Joint Forces Command counterintelligence awareness training (USJFCOM CI), counterinsurgency course, joint antiterrorism course, defense against suicide bombing course, dynamics of international terrorism, homeland security and defense course, the joint special operations task force course (JSOTF), defensive driving course, vehicle emergency drills (battle drills), composite risk management, airborne school, air assault school, and more. Additionally, he graduated from NATO's Combined Joint Operations Center course in Oberammergau Germany, the Air Command and Staff College, and the National Defense University's Joint & Combined Warfighting School. John earned a Bachelor of Arts degree in business management from Towson University in 1990, graduated from Central Michigan University with a Master of Science in Administration degree in 1995, earned a Master of Operational Arts and Science degree from the U.S. Air Force's Air University in 2004, and graduated from the University of Baltimore with a Doctorate in Public Administration in 2013.